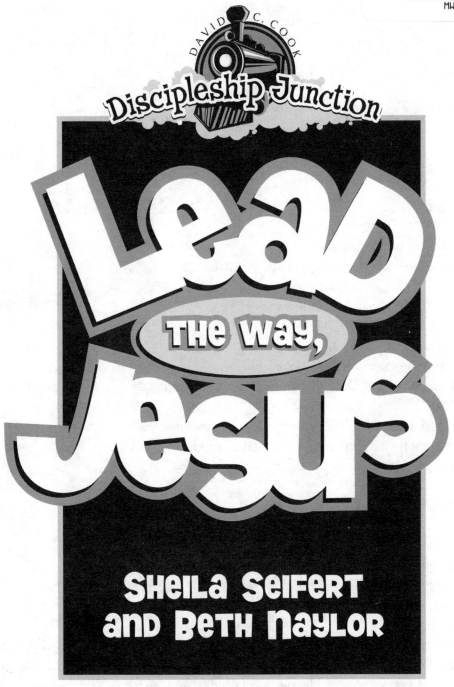

Discipleship Junction

Lead the way, Jesus

Sheila Seifert and Beth Naylor

David C Cook®

transforming lives together

LEAD THE WAY, JESUS
Published by David C Cook
4050 Lee Vance View
Colorado Springs, CO 80918 USA

David C Cook Distribution Canada
55 Woodslee Avenue, Paris, Ontario, Canada N3L 3E5

David C Cook U.K., Kingsway Communications
Eastbourne, East Sussex BN23 6NT, England

Cover Design: BMB Design/Scott Johnson
Cover Illustration: BMB Design/Ryan Putnam
Interior Design: Sandy Flewelling, TrueBlue Design
Interior Illustrations: Aline Heiser

ISBN 978-0-7814-4560-3

First Printing 2008
Printed in the United States of America

3 4 5 6 7 8 9 10 11 12

091710

Table of Contents

Welcome to *Discipleship Junction!* 4

Lesson 1:   Jesus—Favored by God and Man · Luke 2:41–52 6
Like Jesus, we can grow up pleasing God and our parents.

Lesson 2:   Jesus, the Servant · Matthew 20:20–28 12
Like Jesus, we can serve others with caring hearts.

Lesson 3:   Jesus, Teaching Truth · Luke 6:43–45 18
Jesus wants us to know and live the truth.

Lesson 4:   Jesus, the Miracle Maker · Luke 17:11–19 24
We owe Jesus gratefulness and praise.

Lesson 5:   Jesus, Always Kind · Matthew 20:29–34 30
Like Jesus, we can show kindness.

Lesson 6:   Jesus—Build Wealth in Heaven · Luke 12:15–21 36
Love God more than your stuff.

Lesson 7:   Jesus, the Healer · John 5:2–9 42
Like Jesus, we can show mercy.

Lesson 8:   Jesus' New Commandments · Matthew 22:35–40 48
Love Jesus first, and others next.

Lesson 9:   Jesus Deserves Honor · John 12:1–8 54
Let's honor Jesus with our best.

Lesson 10: Jesus Leaves a Reminder · Luke 22:7–20 60
We remember what Jesus did for us.

Lesson 11: Jesus Suffered and Died · Luke 22:47—23:49 66
Jesus loves us so much that he died for us.

Lesson 12: Jesus—Alive Again! · Mark 15:42—16:8; Luke 23:50—24:12 72
Jesus showed us his power when he rose from the dead.

Lesson 13: Jesus—Coming Again! · Acts 1:9–11; 1 Thessalonians 4:15–17; 5:1–2 78
Jesus is coming again!

RESOURCES 84

WELCOME TO DISCIPLESHIP JUNCTION!

Discipleship Junction is an all-new program that harnesses the power of FUN to build young disciples through interaction with Bible Truth and with each other.

A complete, multi-age children's ministry program, Discipleship Junction is packed full of interactive stories and drama, Scripture memory, and themed snacks and activities that will engage every child! It is guaranteed effective because its principles and methods of instruction are teacher-tested and kid-approved!

Intensive student-teacher interaction within a learning community that is relational and supportive makes Discipleship Junction an ideal program for including children with disabilities. Hands-on learning activities are easily adapted to include all students. For more ideas about inclusion, an excellent resource is *Let All the Children Come to Me* by MaLesa Breeding, Ed.D.; Dana Hood, Ph.D.; and Jerry Whitworth, Ed.D. (Colorado Springs: David C.Cook, 2006).

PUTTING THE PIECES TOGETHER

Get Set. We know you're busy, so we provide a list of materials and what you'll need to prepare for your lesson. You'll also need a photocopy machine and some basic classroom supplies: paper, pencils, markers, butcher paper, scissors, glue, and index cards. When you see this icon 🕰 allow a little extra prep time.

Kids love to dress up! Many of our Bible lessons use costume props from the Bible time dress-up box. This can be as simple as a box of items you gather from around the house or purchase inexpensively from a second-hand store. It should include: fake beard, swords, headcloths and browbands, bathrobes, modern-day dress-ups, crown, decorative chains and belts, etc.

Tickets Please! *(10 minutes).* Each week begins with an activity option to involve children while parents are dropping others off.
- *The Welcome Time Activity* will excite children's interest and help them connect with the Bible Truth for the week.

All Aboard for Bible Truth! *(20 minutes).* Whole group, interactive Bible lessons invite students ages 6 to 11 to participate in the entire lesson. Whether it's role-playing Zacchaeus or running a feather relay, kids will be engaged in exciting, hands-on lessons.
- Pre- and post-lesson discussion times encourage children to talk about their own life experiences and tie their knowledge to the week's Bible Truth.
- *Use the Clues!* Practice is an important part of learning, and helps us move information from short-term to long-term memory. *Lead the Way, Jesus* uses the exciting theme of a fun game show—complete with a Game Show Wheel—to help children practice and apply what they have learned. At the end of every lesson you'll play an exciting Game Show to go over the lesson focus. In the weeks that follow, students are repeatedly challenged to remember the Bible Truths by spinning the Game Show Wheel and answering the questions in true game show fashion, including some exciting "bonus" fun if they spin the "bonus" color!

Bible Memory Waypoint *(5 minutes).* Toe tappin' and finger snappin'...there's nothing like the power of FUN to motivate children. Movement, rhythm, and role-play make it easy for kids to hide God's Word in their hearts (Psalm 119:11).

Prayer Station (*15 minutes*). Small-group prayer time for children. Wow! What an idea! Children break into small groups of three to five with an adult helper—we call them StationMasters. Using reproducible instruction cards, adults guide children to explore and practice new prayer skills. Together they'll share concerns, praise God, and practice the four activities of prayer using the imPACT model: *Praise, Ask, Confess, Thank.*

(*Optional*) **Snack Stop and Activities** (*10 minutes*). Tied to the theme of the lesson, you have options for snacks and activities in which lesson truths are practiced and shared. Look for the throttle icon that shows the level of mess, energy, or noise required for the activity!

On the Fast Track! Reproducible take-home pages invite families to interact in and through fun activities and Bible memory.

Are you looking for an additional way to motivate young learners? Discipleship Junction includes an optional incentive program that rewards students for completing take-home pages. Children return a signed *Fast Track!* ticket and choose a prize from the treasure box. If you have a new student, you might welcome that child with the choice of a treasure too! Simply cover and decorate a large shoebox. Fill with inexpensive items such as you might find at a party store.

HOW TO GET STARTED

1. **Begin by recruiting StationMasters**—adult helpers who will guide children through the process of praying in small groups. Don't have enough adult volunteers? How about recruiting middle- or high-school students to shepherd a group? Also consider enlisting a few faithful prayer partners who will commit to praying for your class weekly.

Plan to have a brief training session with your volunteers in which you'll explain how to use the imPACT model of prayer. Each week you'll give the StationMasters a reproducible instruction card with the day's prayer theme and prayer suggestions to use with children in a small group.

2. **Set up your room.** You'll need a big area for your large-group Bible teaching time. You'll also need to identify spaces for each of your small prayer groups. Don't forget that moving chairs and tables, or moving groups to a hallway is always an option. And children are willing helpers!

3. **Photocopy reproducibles** (see Resources) for StationMasters and parents. Mail these two or three weeks before you begin your children's ministry program. Photocopy *On the Fast Track!* pages for each child, and *StationMaster Cards* for each adult helper. If you choose, make copies of the reproducibles for all the lessons ahead of time. This can save a last-minute scramble when time is tight!

4. **Prepare the Game Show Wheel and questions board.** Get two white foam-core sheets. Using a homemade compass (see Resources), you will make a multi-colored, six-section wheel to mount on a wall in your teaching area. For the Game Show Wheel questions board, color six envelopes to match the wheel colors, one envelope per color and pin up on a colorful foam board or bulletin board (see Resources). Each week you will photocopy that week's questions from *Use the Clues!* and place one in each colored envelope.

5. Gather and prepare your materials, set out your snacks, and you are ready to roll. So ... **FULL SPEED AHEAD! ALL ABOARD FOR DISCIPLESHIP JUNCTION!**

Memory Verse:
Teach me your way, O LORD, and I will walk in your truth (Psalm 86:11).

Bible Basis:
Luke 2:41–52

Bible Truth:
Like Jesus, we can grow up pleasing God and our parents.

You Will Need:

- [ ] poster board
- [ ] Game Show Wheel
- [ ] Game Show envelope board
- [ ] construction paper
- [ ] masking tape
- [ ] various toys for babies through 10-year-olds, such as teething ring, rattle, stuffed animal, toy blocks, doll, play dough, superhero figure, flying disk
- [ ] sack or cloth bag
- [ ] blindfold
- [ ] *On the Fast Track! #1* take-home paper
- [ ] *StationMaster Card #1*
- [ ] *(Optional)* treasure box
- [ ] *(Optional)* snack: graham crackers, icing, plastic knives
- [ ] *(Optional)* Activity #2: construction paper, pencils, scissors, markers

When you see this icon, it means preparation will take more than five minutes.

GET SET!
(Lesson Preparation)

- ■ Print today's Bible memory verse on a poster board: **Teach me your way, O LORD, and I will walk in your truth (Psalm 86:11).** Hang the board on the wall.
- ■ Place the toys in the bag and set it out along with the blindfold for the Welcome Time Activity.
- ■ Write the memory verse on construction paper, one word per sheet (including the reference). Tape to the floor in a winding pathway.
- ■ Photocopy *On the Fast Track #1* take-home paper for each child.
- ■ Photocopy *StationMaster Card #1* for each helper.
- ■ Set out the Game Show Wheel, Game Show envelope board, and *(optional)* treasure box.
- ■ Set up snack or outside play activities if you include these items in your children's ministry.

TICKETS PLEASE!
(Welcome and Bible Connection)

- ■ ***Objective:*** *To excite children's interest and connect their own life experiences with the Bible Truth, children will identify toys by touch and talk about at what age they would use that kind of toy.*

Welcome Time Activity: Touch-and-Feel Toy Test

■ *Materials: various toys for babies through 10-year-olds: teething ring, rattle, stuffed animal, toy blocks, doll, play dough, superhero figure, flying disk; sack or cloth bag; blindfold*

As children arrive, direct them to the adult or teen helper with the bag of toys. Children can take turns being blindfolded and reaching into the bag to take out a toy. They'll use their hands to try to identify the toy. After the child has guessed the toy, ask at what age a child might play with that toy. Helpers should stimulate discussion by asking children about how their skills and interests change as they grow up.

Sharing Time and Bible Connection

Introduce today's lesson by discussing these questions with the children. As you talk, give every child the opportunity to say something.

■ **What kinds of feelings do you have?** (happy, sad, excited, afraid, worried, mad, tired, etc.) Write these on the whiteboard as children suggest them.
■ **What kinds of feelings does a mother have?** (the same ones)
■ **Show me how your face would look if you got lost from your family in a big crowd, like at a fair or amusement park.** Observe and comment on children's expressions.
■ **How do you think your mother's face would look if you got lost?**

After this sharing time, help your students connect their discussion to the Bible story they are about to hear from Luke 2.

When Jesus was on earth, he grew up like you're growing up. His mother, Mary, probably felt every one of the feelings we thought of. As Jesus grew up, in everything he did, <u>he wanted to please God and Mary and Joseph.</u> Let's find out about a time when Jesus showed how he pleased Joseph and Mary and God while he was a boy.

ALL ABOARD FOR BIBLE TRUTH
(Bible Discover and Learn Time)

Luke 2:41–52

■ **Objective:** *Children will study Luke 2 and hear an incident from Jesus' childhood that showed how he grew up with the desire to please God and Mary and Joseph.*

Pick three children to act out the parts of Mary, Joseph, and Jesus as you tell the story. The rest of the students can act as the traveling crowd and the teachers in Jerusalem, showing the appropriate expressions on their faces when cued.

As I tell you this story from the book of Luke in the Bible, you'll get to be part of the story by showing on your face different feelings. First, show me a feeling you'd have when you're going to a big party. Observe kids' faces. **Yes, you'd be excited and ready for good times.**

In Luke 2, Jesus was about 12 years old. He was traveling with Mary and Joseph, from their little town of Bethlehem to the huge city of Jerusalem. Have three student actors pretend to walk. **They traveled with a big group of friends every year for the Passover festival. It was a great time of feasting, visiting, and new things to see and do.** Have kids show excited faces. Jesus should wait at side of room.

When the festival was over, Jesus' family started back to Bethlehem. It took days to walk back. After the first day of walking, Mary wondered where Jesus was. She didn't see him with his regular friends. She got a little worried. How would she look? Mary and students show worried faces. **It was a big traveling group, so she finally found her husband, Joseph. "Is Jesus with you?" she wanted to know. Joseph was surprised. "No," he told her. "I thought he was with you!"** Observe surprised faces.

Joseph and Mary went from one traveling family to another. **"Is Jesus with you? Have you seen our son since we left Jerusalem?" They asked Jesus' aunts and uncles, his cousins and friends. No one knew where Jesus was.** All shake heads. **Mary and Joseph turned around and walked quickly back to the city. It was a huge place. "Do you think he's still there in Jerusalem?" Mary and Joseph asked each other.**

If you were Joseph and Mary, where would you look for your child in an enormous city full of people, animals, shops, and travelers? Let kids suggest places. **They looked for three days. Mary and Joseph felt desperate and really worried.**

Finally, they spotted him! Jesus should sit with class. **He was in the temple, talking to the religious teachers! Of all places, they hadn't expected to see him there! He was only 12! They rushed up to Jesus and the men who were around him.**

"Son, what are you doing here?" his mother asked. "Do you know how worried we've been? We've been looking everywhere for you and we were so upset!"

Jesus surprised them with his answer. "Why were you searching for me? Didn't you know I would be in my heavenly Father's house?" Jesus was growing up and wanting to please God, his heavenly Father. He wanted to grow in his spiritual life. But he saw that Mary and Joseph were worried. He knew he'd upset them. Jesus was glad to go back to Bethlehem with them. Have three student actors pretend to walk. **The Bible says he was obedient to them. He wanted to please them by being respectful.**

As Jesus continued to grow up, what <u>he wanted to do most was please God and Mary and Joseph</u>**. That's one reason why he's such a great example for us. God wants the very same thing from us. We can** <u>fol-low Jesus' example and choose to please God and our moms and dads too.</u>

Use the Clues!
(Bible Review)

Okay, let's see what you remember. Show the Game Show Wheel. **Every week after our story we'll take turns spinning the Game Show Wheel. Where the wheel stops shows what color question you'll answer. If you spin the "bonus" or "special" sections, you get to do something fun plus answer a question from a past week for double points.**

You can choose teams that will remain the same for all 13 weeks, or create new teams each class session. After setting up teams, have them alternate spinning and answering questions. Award points based on the color.

- **Why did Jesus' family travel to Jerusalem every year?** (to celebrate the Passover festival)
- **Why did Jesus stay in the city?** (he wanted to please God, his heavenly Father, by learning more and talking to the Jewish teachers in the temple)
- **How did Jesus please Mary and Joseph and God?** (he listened and learned from the Jewish teachers and he obeyed and respected Mary and Joseph)
- **How can we please our parents?** (listen, obey, be respectful)
- **How can you and I please God?** (by growing in our spirit, learning about him and living his way, obeying our parents and others in authority over us)
- **How can the memory verse help you grow up to please God and your parents?** (by following God's words and his way, we can please him and obey our parents; God will help us do what pleases him)

Even when he was growing up, <u>Jesus showed us how we can please God and our parents</u>. His example helps us learn to do things his way, so we grow up not just in our bodies, but also in our spirit. You can follow Jesus' example by acting, talking, and having an attitude that pleases God, your mom, and your dad.

BIBLE MEMORY WAYPOINT
(Scripture Memory)

Psalm 86:11

- **Objective:** *Children will hide God's Word in their hearts for guidance, protection, and encouragement.*

Read this week's memory verse from the poster. Point to each word as you read it:

Teach me your way, O LORD, and I will walk in your truth (Psalm 86:11).

After repeating the verse together a couple of times, lead the children on the winding verse path. Have them repeat after you as you say the verse while they're walking the path. Then break into pairs or threes (mixed ages) to walk the path and say the verse as they pass each word. As each group finishes the path, have them cluster around the end and give high fives to the remaining groups as they finish.

PRAYER STATION

■ **Objective:** *Children will explore and practice prayer for themselves in small groups.*
■ **Materials:** *Copies of* StationMaster Card #1 *for each adult or teen helper*

Break into small groups of three to five children. Assign a teen or adult helper to each small group and give each helper a copy of *StationMaster Card #1* (see Resources) with ideas for group discussion and prayer.

 ## SNACK STOP: GRAHAM CRACKER BOOKS (Optional)

If you plan to provide a snack, this is an ideal time to serve it.

■ **Materials:** *graham crackers, icing, plastic knives*

Have children break their graham crackers into four rectangles and spread icing between segments like a book. As they eat, explain that teachers of the law in Jesus' time studied the Scriptures, which were made up of a lot of books. Talk about what the kids have learned recently from books, and how the Bible is our most valuable book because it teaches how to grow up pleasing God and parents.

Note: Always be aware of children with food allergies and have another option on hand if necessary.

APPLICATION

■ **Objective:** *Children will have opportunities to show how the lesson works in their own lives through activities and take-home papers.*

Some children's ministries may allow children to play outside at this point. If yours does not, choose one of the following activities.

Watch and Learn

Explain to children that we learn to please parents and God by following Jesus' example. Divide the class into two or more groups. Form front-to-back lines, with everyone but the first player in each line facing the back of the line. You'll start the game by silently demonstrating an action that the first player in each line must learn from your example. Choose a silly action, like patting your head while rubbing your tummy, or a sequence of moves like touching toes, knees, hips, and then flapping your arms. Once learned, the player taps the next child in line, who will turn around and learn the action by example. (You may need to move groups apart so they don't see each other's actions.) First group finished wins. Have last players in each group demonstrate what they learned: **How well did they learn by example? What actions and attitudes did Jesus show that we should be learning?** (kindness, unselfishness, love, gentleness, obedience to parents, listening, seeking to learn God's Word, being a good friend, patience, etc.)

Follow-through Footprints

■ *Materials: construction paper, pencils, scissors, markers*

Have children pair up to trace each other's feet so each child ends up with two paper footprints (with or without shoes). They'll cut out their foot shapes. On one, the child will write or draw a way they can behave or words they can choose to show they are doing something pleasing to a parent. On the other foot shape, they'll write or draw something that would please God. Encourage realistic, original thinking (do my chores right the first time, or play nice with my little sister; talk to God every night before bed, or try not to call my brother a name when I'm mad).

ON THE FAST TRACK! *(Take-Home Papers)*

■ *Materials:* On the Fast Track! #1, *treasure box*

(Optional) Introduce the treasure box by asking: **Who would like to choose a prize from the treasure box?** Anticipate excited responses. Show *On the Fast Track!* take-home papers. **When you take this *On the Fast Track!* paper home each week and do the activities, your parents can sign the ticket that you finished the work. Bring the signed ticket back to choose a prize from the treasure box.** Distribute the take-home papers just before children leave.

Memory Verse:
Serve wholeheartedly, as if you were serving the Lord, not men (Ephesians 6:7).

Bible Basis:
Matthew 20:20–28

Bible Truth:
Like Jesus, we can serve others with caring hearts.

Serve Others and Care

You Will Need:

- [ ] Game Show Wheel
- [ ] Game Show envelope board
- [ ] 1 poster board
- [ ] 8 sheets of paper
- [ ] Large self-adhesive or double-tape-backed gold stars
- [ ] *On the Fast Track! #2* take-home paper
- [ ] *StationMaster Card #2*
- [ ] *(Optional)* treasure box
- [ ] *(Optional)* snack: crackers, spreadable cheese, plastic knives
- [ ] *(Optional)* Activity #1: Bible time dress-up box, additional dress-up items such as caps, gloves, shoes
- [ ] *(Optional)* Activity #2: hemp cord or box twine cut in 18" lengths (three lengths per child)

 When you see this icon, it means preparation will take more than five minutes.

 GET SET!
(Lesson Preparation)

- ◻ Print today's Bible memory verse on a poster board: **Serve wholeheartedly, as if you were serving the Lord, not men (Ephesians 6:7).** Hang the poster board on the wall.
- ◻ Write in these titles on nine separate sheets of paper: king, master, slave, rich ruler, prince, servant, princess, commander.
- ◻ Photocopy *On the Fast Track #2* take-home paper for each child.
- ◻ Photocopy *StationMaster Card #2* for each helper.
- ◻ Set out the Game Show Wheel, Game Show envelope board, and *(optional)* treasure box.
- ◻ Set up snack or outside play activities if you include these items in your children's ministry.
- ◻ Braid a headband before class as a sample, if using the Activity #2.

TICKETS PLEASE!
(Welcome and Bible Connection)

■ **Objective:** *To excite children's interest and connect their own life experiences with the Bible Truth, children will test their serving skills by helping set up the room.*

Welcome Time Activity: Room Setup

■ *Materials: large gold stars*

As children arrive, assign each child or pair of children to a specific task to help prepare the classroom, such as setting up chairs, getting out/sorting dress-up box items, getting out the Game Show Wheel, etc. As each completes a task, attach a gold star to the child's shirt or dress, thanking each child for serving so willingly.

Sharing Time and Bible Connection

Introduce today's lesson by discussing these questions with the class. As you talk, give every child the opportunity to say something.

Ask for eight volunteers and give each a sheet with a job title printed on it.

■ **What order should these helpers stand in, based on their title?** Allow sitting students to suggest the "pecking order."

■ **Why did you choose this order for these titles?**

■ **Which of these titles do you think deserves the most honor? Why?**

■ **Which title do you think most people would choose if they had a choice?**

After this sharing time, help your students connect their discussion to the Bible story they are about to hear from Matthew 20.

I think the list you made and the reasons you gave are what most people would say. Everyone wants to have the best job and the top title. Usually there's more honor and privilege in the top jobs. But sometimes the people at the top don't care about those under them. In the Bible story we're about to study, we'll find out that, <u>like Jesus, we can serve others with caring hearts</u>.

ALL ABOARD FOR BIBLE TRUTH
(Bible Discover and Learn Time)

Matthew 20: 20–28

■ **Objective:** *Children will study Matthew 20:20–28 and find out that Jesus came as a servant.*

Show children how to "rock" a baby each time you say "mother." Have children hold up two fingers when you say "sons." When Jesus is mentioned, have students raise their pointer finger over their heads to say #1. You may need to prompt them as needed throughout the story.

In the book of Matthew, we read about a mother who was really proud of her two grown-up sons, James and John, who were followers of Jesus. Because she wanted good things for James and John, she made up her mind to ask Jesus a favor. So she got up her courage and came to him. This mother knelt down in front of Jesus, to show her humility. She knew Jesus was from heaven and that he would be a great king.

"What do you want?" Jesus asked her.

This mother asked him, "Please let my two sons sit next to you, one on your right and the other on your left, when you enter your kingdom." This mother knew that if her sons were next to Jesus, it was the very best place for them. After all, what mom wouldn't want her sons to be the closest friends of a powerful king?

She waited for Jesus' answer.

Jesus said, "You have no idea what you're asking. I don't think they can go through what I'm going to have to go through." Do you think the mother and the two sons knew what Jesus was trying to tell them? (probably not) What was Jesus saying he would have to go through? (be crucified and suffer before dying)

"We can," said her sons. They thought it was a perfect plan, having the closest places of honor next to Jesus.

Jesus nodded. "Okay, you will go through the same kind of thing I'll have to go through. But I can't promise where you'll sit in my kingdom. Only God the Father can do that."

Now remember that Jesus had 12 disciples. The other 10 heard what James and John's mother had asked of Jesus. Those 10 were pretty mad about it. Why should James and John get the best honors?

But Jesus was upset at all the complaining and arguing his disciples were doing. So he called them together.

What Jesus said really surprised them. He said, "The way the world works is that everyone has someone over him, telling him what to do. In this world, the most powerful rule over those who are weaker. But my kingdom isn't like that at all. If you want to be great, you must serve other people. Whoever wants to be first has to serve others. I didn't come to live on earth so I could rule over people.

I came to be an example by the way I serve you. And the most important way I'm going to serve you is to give my life for you."

Jesus told the disciples and us that <u>he came to serve, and that's the example we're to follow</u>.

Use the Clues!
(Bible Review)

Okay, let's see what you remember. Show the Game Show Wheel. **Every week after our story we'll take turns spinning the Game Show Wheel. The color the wheel stops at shows what color question you'll answer. If you spin the "bonus" or "special" sections, you get to do something fun plus answer a question for double points.**

■ **What did the mother ask Jesus?** (to give places of honor to her sons, to let James and John have the right and left places next to Jesus in his kingdom)

■ **What did Jesus come to earth for?** (to serve us and to give his life to pay for our sin, so we can have a friendship with God)

■ **What did Jesus promise if we become willing servants to others?** (the first will be last, those who serve are the greatest in his kingdom)

■ **How can kids like you serve others?** Accept reasonable responses.

■ **What does the memory verse teach about serving?** (serve with all your heart like you're doing it just for God)

■ (Review question) **What did Jesus teach us from his example of growing up?** (to aim to please God and our parents)

Jesus lived on earth so we could know God. He taught us the most important things by the way he lived. In this story, Jesus explained that being great isn't a position or title. It's the way you follow his example by serving the people around you.

BIBLE MEMORY WAYPOINT   Ephesians 6:7
(Scripture Memory)

■ ***Objective:*** *Children will hide God's Word in their hearts for guidance, protection, and encouragement.*

Read this week's memory verse from the poster. Point to each word as you read it:

Serve wholeheartedly, as if you were serving the Lord, not men (Ephesians 6:7).

Repeat the memory verse several times so children become familiar with it. Play Popcorn to continue the memorization. With everyone sitting in a circle, start the game by popping up to stand and say two words of the verse, then sit. The person to your left pops up to say the next two words, then sits. Continue around the circle, repeating the verse. Reverse directions, and invert the "pop" with everyone standing and crouching for their turn. Try to get the verse flowing smoothly and the popping moving rapidly.

PRAYER STATION

- **Objective:** *Children will explore and practice prayer for themselves in small groups.*
- **Materials:** *Copies of* StationMaster Card #2 *for each adult or teen helper*

Break into small groups of three to five children. Assign a teen or adult helper to each small group and give each helper a copy of *StationMaster Card #2* (see Resources) with ideas for group discussion and prayer.

SNACK STOP: SERVANT SANDWICHES (Optional)

If you plan to provide a snack, this is an ideal time to serve it.

- **Materials:** *crackers, spreadable cheese, plastic knives*

Invite children to practice their serving skills by helping assemble cracker sandwiches. Assign different jobs to pairs of students, including cleaning the table, putting away supplies, and giving thanks for the snack.

Note: Always be aware of children with food allergies and have another option on hand if necessary.

APPLICATION

- **Objective:** *Children will have opportunities to show how the lesson works in their own lives through activities and take-home papers.*

Some children's ministries may allow children to play outside at this point. If yours does not, choose one of the following activities.

Garment Getup

■ *Materials: Bible time dress-up box, plus additional items such as caps, gloves, shoes*

This game needs lots of servants! Divide into teams as needed for class size. Choose a "master" from each team and station him/her in the center of the team circle next to a box or bag of dress-up items. Each bag should contain five items of clothing. At the starting signal, one team member from the circle chooses a clothing item and puts it on the "master" as best he can, then returns to his place so the next team member can take a turn adding a piece of clothing. Emphasize that the servants should take care to make their master look as good as possible. First team to fully outfit the master wins. **Who are you really serving anytime you serve someone?** (God)

Servant Headbands

■ *Materials: hemp cord or box twine cut in 18" lengths (three lengths per child)*

Pair up children so an older one works with a younger one. One child holds one end of the three cords while the other braids. Demonstrate how to braid the three lengths of cord, then have children work in pairs to help each other braid. Knot the lengths together at one end before starting and finish with a knot at the other end. Have children wrap the braid around their head like a headband that a servant in Bible times might have worn. Challenge kids to wear or carry the headband this week to prompt them to serve someone each day.

ON THE FAST TRACK! *(Take-Home Papers)*

■ *Materials: On the Fast Track! #2, treasure box*

(*Optional*) Introduce the treasure box by asking: **Who would like to choose a prize from the treasure box?** Anticipate excited responses. Show *On the Fast Track!* take-home papers. **When you take this *On the Fast Track!* paper home each week and do the activities, your parents can sign the ticket that you finished the work. Bring the signed ticket back to choose a prize from the treasure box.** Distribute the take-home papers just before children leave.

Know and Live the Truth

Memory Verse:

Your word is truth (John 17:17).

Bible Basis:

Luke 6:43–45

Bible Truth:

Jesus wants us to know and live the truth.

You Will Need:

- [ ] Game Show Wheel
- [ ] Game Show envelope board
- [ ] 1 poster board
- [ ] cardstock
- [ ] markers
- [ ] tape
- [ ] two tree branches, one healthy and one dried out
- [ ] a thorn branch
- [ ] towel
- [ ] one good orange and one old, hard orange or shriveled piece of peel
- [ ] tape or safety pins
- [ ] *On the Fast Track! #3* take-home paper
- [ ] *StationMaster Card #3*
- [ ] *(Optional)* treasure box
- [ ] *(Optional)* snack: short skewers (or toothpicks) of fruit chunks (apples, grapes, melon, pineapple, etc.)
- [ ] *(Optional)* Activity #2: rope or tape

When you see this icon, it means preparation will take more than five minutes.

GET SET!

(Lesson Preparation)

- Print today's Bible memory verse on a poster board: **Your word is truth (John 17:17).** Hang the poster board on the wall.
- Cut the cardstock into four equal-sized quarters if using the Welcome Time Activity, making at least 12 quarters.
- For the Bible lesson, bring in two actual tree branches, about three feet long, or make them from a stick and paper for leaves. One branch should be healthy with plenty of fresh leaves; the other should have mostly shriveled, diseased, or dead leaves.
- Cut two lengths of string each about six inches long. Knot each at one end and attach each to an orange using a tack or heavy-duty pin. Tie a small loop at the opposite ends and attach a large paper clip, bent open, as a hanger for each orange.
- Wrap the thorn branch securely with a towel at one end, and tape the towel in place as a handle.
- Photocopy *On the Fast Track #3* take-home paper for each child.
- Photocopy *StationMaster Card #3* for each helper.
- Set out the Game Show Wheel, Game Show envelope board, and *(optional)* treasure box.
- Set up snack or outside play activities if you include these items in your children's ministry.
- For next week's Bible story, photocopy the script on pages 26–27. Ask a teen or adult man to prepare for dramatizing the role of the healed leper from Luke 17:11–19. Learn the reporter's lines as well as possible in advance also.

TICKETS PLEASE!
(Welcome and Bible Connection)

■ *Objective:* To excite children's interest and connect their own life experiences with the Bible Truth, children will play a matching game and talk about how to identify good fruit.

Welcome Time Activity: Fruit Matching Game
■ *Materials:* cardstock, markers, tape

As children arrive, engage them in a game of matching. Ask the first several children to draw cards of different kinds of fruit. They should make sets of two cards of the same fruit. After several children have arrived to play the game, attach a card to each child's back. Make sure there are two of each fruit playing (no single fruit cards). The children have to find the person who has the fruit that matches theirs by giving descriptive clues (color, shape, taste, size, etc.) of what's on the other's back. Talk about how to know if a piece of fruit is good or not (color, size, smell, etc.).

Sharing Time and Bible Connection

Introduce today's lesson by discussing these questions with the children. As you talk, give every child the opportunity to say something.

■ **What kinds of fruit have you seen growing?**
■ **If you had a pear tree in your yard, what would you expect to grow on that tree?** (pears)
■ **What do you think you might find on a tree that hasn't been watered or has been ruined by insects and not taken care of?** (bad fruit, no fruit, fruit that doesn't taste good)

After this sharing time, help your students connect their discussion to the Bible story they are about to hear from Luke 6.

You're right that an apple tree will always grow apples, and a pear tree will always grow pears. A tree that gets no water and has bugs all over it won't have fruit that's good to eat. Jesus used good fruit and bad fruit to teach us about being truthful in our lives. Let's see what he said.

ALL ABOARD FOR BIBLE TRUTH
(Bible Discover and Learn Time)

Luke 6:43-45

■ **Objective:** *Children will study Luke 6 to discover that Jesus wants them to live lives of truthfulness inside and out.*

■ **Materials:** *good and bad tree branches, thorn branch with one end wrapped securely with a towel, two oranges with string hangers attached*

Ask for three volunteers to join you standing in front of the group.

Jesus taught people a lot about God and living God's way. He sometimes used parables. These are stories that teach us something important. One parable he told was about good fruit and bad fruit.

Hand one volunteer the lush-looking tree branch. **Let's say _____** (child's name) **is a good orange tree. Jesus said that a good tree grows good fruit. How would you know this is a good tree?** (it's green, tall, has lots of leaves, produces lots of oranges) Hang a good-looking orange from the branch. **Because this tree is so healthy, well-watered, and pruned, it grows good fruit. The tree has to be good on the inside, not just the outside, to make good fruit. Every year we can expect to pick tasty, juicy oranges from this tree.**

Hand the second volunteer the broken branch with dead leaves. **_____** (child's name) **is a bad orange tree. How do we know this tree isn't a good one?** (it's dried up, dead looking, old) **This tree looks bad because it IS bad, from the inside out. So what kind of fruit do you expect this tree to have?** (bad or no fruit) Hang the shriveled orange from the branch. **Every year this tree would have less and less fruit, and it wouldn't be anything you could eat.**

Hand the last volunteer the wrapped end of the thorn branch. **What is this?** Allow children to answer. **Jesus said no one picks tasty figs from a thorn bush. And you wouldn't find fat, juicy grapes hanging from a sticker bush, would you?**

What do you think Jesus was trying to tell us with this good tree, bad tree story? Accept responses. **Jesus said people are like trees in some ways. A good person is going to have good things coming out of him. Someone who lives God's way will have good actions and speak only things that are true. Good things come out of people who are good inside, where God's Spirit lives. But people who choose not to live God's way show bad habits and words. They lie, trick people, try to do what's good only for themselves, and aren't honest. A bad person doesn't have the truthful character of a good person. A bad person can't help but show bad actions, because the truth of God isn't inside him or her.**

Just like you can't expect to get a basket of sweet cherries from a sticker bush, a person who doesn't live for God won't be able to speak truth or live honestly. Good actions come from a person whose heart chooses to do things God's way.

Jesus pointed out to us with a picture of good fruit (point to good tree) **and bad fruit** (point to bad tree) **that the way we live shows what's inside of us. And he wants us to <u>follow his example of knowing and living the truth</u>.**

Use the Clues!
(Bible Review)

Okay, let's see what you remember. Show the Game Show Wheel. Every week after our story we'll take turns spinning the Game Show Wheel. The color the wheel stops at shows what color question you'll answer. If you spin the "bonus" or "special" sections, you get to do something fun plus answer a question for double points.

■ **What does the good tree stand for in Jesus' parable?** (a person who lives God's way and has good actions and truthful words)

■ **Why can't a tree with dried-up branches produce good fruit?** (it's bad from the inside out, it has nothing that lets it make fruit)

■ **Why can't a bad person pretend to be good and look just like a good person?** (whatever is inside him comes out in the way he acts and talks)

■ **How can we live a life that is full of truth?** (follow Jesus and live God's way)

■ **Whose example will guide us in knowing and living the truth?** (Jesus')

■ **What is truth, according to our memory verse?** (God's Word)

BIBLE MEMORY WAYPOINT   John 17:17
(Scripture Memory)

■ *Objective: Children will hide God's Word in their hearts for guidance, protection, and encouragement.*

Read this week's memory verse from the poster. Point to each word as you read it:
Your word is truth (John 17:17).

To help children memorize the verse, teach a truth cheer. Call out, "Give me a T!" The students should shout back, "T!" Do this for all the letters of the word "truth." Then ask, "What does it spell?" The kids should respond, "Truth!" Recite the verse together and let a couple of kids lead the truth cheer again.

PRAYER STATION

- ■ **Objective:** *Children will explore and practice prayer for themselves in small groups.*
- ■ **Materials:** *Copies of* StationMaster Card #3 *for each adult or teen helper*

Break the large group into smaller groups of three to five children. Assign a teen or adult helper to each small group and give each helper a copy of *StationMaster Card #3* (see Resources) with ideas for group discussion and prayer.

SNACK STOP: FRUIT KABOBS (Optional)

If you plan to provide a snack, this is an ideal time to serve it.

- ■ **Materials:** *short skewers (or toothpicks) of fruit chunks (apples, grapes, melon, bananas, pineapple, etc.)*

As children eat their fruit kabobs, ask them for examples of how our actions can be truthful or not truthful, just like our words.

Note: Always be aware of children with food allergies and have another option on hand if necessary.

APPLICATION

- ■ **Objective:** *Children will have opportunities to show how the lesson works in their own lives through activities and take-home papers.*

Some children's ministries may allow children to play outside at this point. If yours does not, choose one of the following activities.

Fruit Basket Upset

Set chairs in a circle, with one fewer than the number of players. Ask one volunteer to start in the middle of the chair circle. Walk around the circle and randomly assign children one of three or four different fruits (such as kiwi, bananas, grapes, apples). To play, call out one type of fruit. All with that fruit name leap from their chairs and scramble to find and sit in another open chair. The child in the center tries to reach an open chair and becomes the type of fruit that was just called. Whoever is left standing without a seat takes the center place. You can choose to have the one unseated child be the caller of the fruit names. After several rounds, you can assign new fruit names.

 ## Good Fruit, Bad Fruit Jump
■ *Materials: rope or tape*

Lay the rope or tape down the middle of the play area, long enough so that the children can line up along it with some space between them. Have all children start on the same side, facing forward. Explain that the side they're standing on is the "good fruit" side. The opposite side is the "bad fruit" side. You'll call out actions and words that are good or bad, and they will have to jump or not jump to be on the side that matches your command. Those who jump the wrong way sit out until the next round. Randomly call out "good" actions and words such as truthful, honest, fair, and "bad" ones such as lying, cheating, false, unfair. Speed up the calls to make the game more challenging. The winner is the final player left playing.

 ## ON THE FAST TRACK! *(Take-Home Papers)*

■ *Materials:* On the Fast Track! #3, *treasure box*

(Optional) Introduce the treasure box by asking: **Who would like to choose a prize from the treasure box?** Anticipate excited responses. Show *On the Fast Track!* take-home papers. **When you take this *On the Fast Track!* paper home each week and do the activities, your parents can sign the ticket that you finished the work. Bring the signed ticket back to choose a prize from the treasure box.** Distribute the take-home papers just before children leave.

Memory Verse:
Give thanks to the LORD, for he is good. His love endures forever (Psalm 136:1).

Bible Basis:
Luke 17:11–19

Bible Truth:
We owe Jesus gratefulness and praise.

You Will Need:

- [ ] Game Show Wheel
- [ ] Game Show envelope board
- [ ] Bible time dress-up box
- [ ] 1 poster board
- [ ] dowels or sticks
- [ ] fabric or regular markers
- [ ] rectangles and triangles of light-colored fabric or heavy paper
- [ ] lively praise CD
- [ ] CD player
- [ ] pretend microphone (a foam ball glued to a toilet paper tube)
- [ ] *(Optional)* small notebook
- [ ] *On the Fast Track! #4* take-home paper
- [ ] *StationMaster Card #4*
- [ ] *(Optional)* treasure box
- [ ] *(Optional)* snack: apple slices, grapes, melon chunks, caramel or fruit dip, plastic spoon, paper plates
- [ ] *(Optional)* Activity #1: praise music CD, CD player, praise banners if made in Welcome Time Activity, praise instruments
- [ ] *(Optional)* Activity #2: approximately 6" square stiff, clear acetate sheets, watercolor markers, small round hole punch, nylon string in 12" lengths

 When you see this icon, it means preparation will take more than five minutes.

GET SET!
(Lesson Preparation)

- ■ ⏱ Print today's Bible memory verse on a poster board: **Give thanks to the LORD, for he is good. His love endures forever (Psalm 136:1).** Hang the poster board on the wall at the front of the classroom.
- ■ Photocopy *On the Fast Track #4* for each child.
- ■ Photocopy *StationMaster Card #4* for each helper.
- ■ Set out the Game Show Wheel, Game Show envelope board, and *(optional)* treasure box.
- ■ Set up snack or outside play activities if you include these items in your children's ministry.
- ■ Set up praise CD and CD player near Welcome Time Activity table.
- ■ ⏱ Cut acetate sheets to 6" squares and nylon thread in 12" lengths if using Activity #2.

TICKETS PLEASE!
(Welcome and Bible Connection)

- ■ ***Objective:*** *To excite children's interest and connect their own life experiences with the Bible Truth, children create praise banners and talk about ways to praise God.*

Welcome Time Activity: Praise Banners

■ *Materials:* dowels or sticks, fabric or regular markers, rectangles and triangles of light-colored fabric or heavy paper, lively praise CD, CD player

As children arrive, have the praise music playing near the table. Invite children to the table where materials are available to create praise banners. Children can use fabric or regular markers to write names of God and Jesus, "Praise to God," "We love Jesus," and other words and phrases of praise and thanksgiving on fabric or paper rectangles and triangles. While working, talk about the many ways we can praise God.

Sharing Time and Bible Connection

Introduce today's lesson by discussing these questions. As you talk, give every child the opportunity to say something.

■ **When was the last time you got a gift or had a treat, like getting a new pet?**
■ **What did you say or do for person who gave the gift or treat?** (said thank you, wrote a thank-you note, sent them an e-mail)
■ **Imagine you needed a miracle, like getting better from a terrible accident. Who would you thank if you got the miracle you needed so much?** (God)

After this sharing time, help your students connect their discussion to the Bible story they are about to hear from Luke 17.

When God answers a prayer we've prayed, or helped us in a hard situation, <u>we should give him thanks and praise</u>. Since you can't send God a thank-you card or an e-mail, how would you thank him for what he did for you? Today in the book of Luke, you'll find out what someone did after Jesus helped him in a big way.

ALL ABOARD FOR BIBLE TRUTH   Luke 17:11-19
(Bible Discover and Learn Time)

■ *Objective: Children will study Luke 17 and learn how one man thanked and praised Jesus for a miraculous healing.*
■ *Materials: Bible time dress-up box, pretend microphone, small notebook*

This Bible story is presented as an interview between a reporter and the leper who returned to thank Jesus for healing him. Ideally a male actor has prepared for the role of the leper in advance. If necessary, write your questions inside a small notebook like a reporter might use and refer to them as needed. Have the "leper" dress up using items from the Bible time dress-up box.

Today you're going to hear what happened to a man who lived in the time of Jesus. He had a really bad sickness called leprosy. His skin turned white and hard. Because he was so sick, he had to live outside the city, away from his family. His only friends were other people who also had leprosy. There was no medicine to make them better.

(Leper is rather breathless and very excited.)

Reporter: Sir, I hear you've had something amazing just happen. Can you tell us what's going on?

Leper: You might not believe it, but it's true! I'm all healed!

Reporter: Healed from what?

Leper: Leprosy. *(Reporter makes a nasty face and moves back.)*

Leper: Don't worry, I'm all well now. Jesus healed me. I'm so thankful to Jesus. His awesome power just gave me back my life!

Reporter: Can you tell me exactly what happened?

Leper: I sure will! He didn't even know me, but he cured me. I was outside the city with nine other guys. We live out there alone, because lepers can't go inside the city. But we saw some people coming to the city. They stayed in the village nearby and I heard that Jesus, the Son of God, was there. When they walked down the road, we stood at a distance and called out to Jesus to have mercy on us.

Reporter: Did Jesus give you some special water or touch you or something?

Leper: No. He just told us what to do.

(Long pause) **Reporter:** Well, what was it?

Leper: Jesus just said, "Go show yourself to the priests." We were shocked. A leper can go show his skin to the priest only if he's well. We didn't understand, but we believed Jesus would help us. So we started walking to the city to find the priests. But we didn't even get there and suddenly we were totally well. All the white leprosy spots were just gone.

Reporter: *(incredulous)*: Gone? All of them?

Leper: Totally. We were well! I'm so excited. The first thing I wanted to do was tell Jesus thank you. I ran back to where he was and just fell in front of him. I was too excited to do more than say thank you over and over again.

Reporter: What did Jesus say to the 10 of you?

Leper: 10? No, it was just me.

Reporter: You said there were 10 of you who were sick. You mean only you got cured?

Leper: No, we all were perfectly healthy at the same time. But I was the only one who went back and praised and thanked Jesus.

Reporter: What did Jesus do then?

Leper: He told me to get up and go home. He said my faith had made me well. I knew Jesus was God all along, and that's why he could make me well. I'll never be able to thank him enough. Jesus is great!

(Healed leper walks away praising and thanking Jesus.)

You know that man was just pretending to be the leper from the Bible. But Jesus did heal 10 men. It probably made Jesus sad to see only one show his thanks for such a great miracle. Anytime God shows love toward us, answers a prayer, or gives us what we need, <u>we need to show our thanks and praise to him</u>.

Use the Clues!
(Bible Review)

Okay, let's see what you remember. Show the Game Show Wheel. **Every week after our story we'll take turns spinning the Game Show Wheel. The color the wheel stops at shows what color question you'll answer. If you spin the "bonus" or "special" sections, you get to do something fun plus answer a question for double points.**

- **Why did the lepers ask Jesus for help?** (no one else could heal them, they knew he was the Son of God)
- **What did the one man do after he was healed?** (went back to thank Jesus, kept praising him)
- **How should we act when God has shown love or answered a prayer for us?** (tell him thank you, praise him, be grateful, tell others what God did for us)
- **How can we praise and thank God when he uses his power and acts in love toward us?** (pray, let others know how good God is, sing praise songs)
- **What does our memory verse say about God?** (his love endures forever, he is good)
- (Review question) **What did Jesus teach us about living the truth?** Accept any reasonable answers related to last week's lesson.

The leper is a perfect example for us. He immediately told Jesus thank you and praised him. Other people would hear of Jesus from this man's grateful praises. Just like you say thank you for a birthday gift or a treat someone gives you, God deserves praise and thanks for all he does for us.

BIBLE MEMORY WAYPOINT
Psalm 136:1
(Scripture Memory)

- *Objective: Children will hide God's Word in their hearts for guidance, protection, and encouragement.*

Read this week's memory verse from the poster. Point to each word as you read it:
Give thanks to the LORD, for he is good. His love endures forever (Psalm 136:1).

To help children memorize the Bible verse, create a chant. Divide the class in two. One half will say in unison, "Give thanks to the Lord." The other half will respond, "For he is good." The first half then chants, "His love endures," with the second half finishing with

"Forever." Do this several times until familiar, then switch which group goes first. After each recitation of the verse, everyone says the reference together. If the kids need to move their bodies, add movements to the phrases.

PRAYER STATION

- *Objective:* Children will explore and practice prayer for themselves in small groups.
- *Materials:* Copies of StationMaster Card #4 for each adult or teen helper

Break into small groups of three to five children. Assign a teen or adult helper to each small group and give each helper a copy of *StationMaster Card #4* (see Resources) with ideas for group discussion and prayer.

SNACK STOP: THANKSGIVING DUNKS (Optional)

If you plan to provide a snack, this is an ideal time to serve it.

- *Materials:* apple slices, grapes, melon chunks, caramel dip or other fruit dip, plastic spoon, paper plates

Distribute fruit and a spoonful of dip to each child. Tell kids they can dip the different fruits into the dip, but they need to thank or praise God for each treat they take.

Note: Always be aware of children with food allergies and have another option on hand if necessary.

APPLICATION

- *Objective:* Children will have opportunities to show how the lesson works in their own lives through activities and take-home papers.

Some children's ministries may allow children to play outside at this point. If yours does not, choose one of the following activities.

Praise Parade

■ *Materials: praise music CD, CD player, praise banners if made in Welcome Time Activity, praise instruments*

Praising God can mean being thankful as we pray, telling God how special he is, singing, and clapping. Involve the children in active praise. Play an energetic praise song that the children know or can begin to learn. Give them freedom to move their bodies, kneel in praise, or clap. If desired, create a praise parade. Use banners made in the Welcome Time Activity, praise instruments, or other materials in the classroom.

Praise Light Catchers

■ *Materials: approximately 6" square, stiff, clear acetate sheets, watercolor markers, small round hole punch, nylon string in 12" lengths*

Children will make light catchers that can be mounted in a sunny window as a reminder to praise God often. Using watercolor markers, children will write praise words—"I love you, Jesus," "God is good," "God's love endures forever," etc.—on an acetate square. They can add doodles and decorations too. Hole punch about ¼" from each top corner. Thread and knot an end of a length of nylon thread into the two holes as a hanger. Avoid getting wet, as marker will smudge and run.

ON THE FAST TRACK! *(Take-Home Papers)*

■ *Materials: On the Fast Track! #4, treasure box*

(Optional) Introduce the treasure box by asking: **Who would like to choose a prize from the treasure box?** Anticipate excited responses. Show *On the Fast Track!* take-home papers. **When you take this *On the Fast Track!* paper home each week and do the activities, your parents can sign the ticket that you finished the work. Bring the signed ticket back to choose a prize from the treasure box.** Distribute the take-home papers just before children leave.

LESSON FIVE: Jesus, Always Kind

Memory Verse:

Make sure that nobody pays back wrong for wrong, but **always try to be kind to each other and to everyone else** (1 Thessalonians 5:15).

*Note: Younger children may memorize the shorter version of this verse in **bold** print.*

Bible Basis:

Matthew 20:29–34

Bible Truth:

Like Jesus, we can show kindness.

You Will Need:

- [ ] Game Show Wheel
- [ ] Game Show envelope board
- [ ] 1 poster board
- [ ] *(Optional)* blindfolds
- [ ] simple puzzles
- [ ] beanbag, numbered papers
- [ ] Bibles, pencils, paper
- [ ] *On the Fast Track! #5* take-home paper
- [ ] *StationMaster Card #5*
- [ ] *(Optional)* treasure box
- [ ] *(Optional)* snack: oaten-ring cereal, licorice strings or cloth string cut in 14" lengths
- [ ] *(Optional)* Activity #2: cardstock, thick markers, photocopied bingo images from page 84, glue sticks, scissors, small objects for bingo markers

 GET SET!

(Lesson Preparation)

- ■ Print today's Bible memory verse on a poster board: **Make sure that nobody pays back wrong for wrong, but always try to be kind to each other and to everyone else (1 Thessalonians 5:15).** Hang the poster board on the wall at the front of the classroom.
- ■ Photocopy *On the Fast Track #5* for each child.
- ■ Photocopy *StationMaster Card #5* for each helper.
- ■ Make up numbered sheets from 3 to 24, using multiples of 3 (3, 6, 9, 12, etc.) for the Bible Memory activity.
- ■ Photocopy the Kindness Bingo images from page 84.
- ■ Prepare a sample Kindness Bingo card with nine marker-drawn sections if using Activity #2.
- ■ Set out the Game Show Wheel, Game Show envelope board, and *(optional)* treasure box.
- ■ Set up snack or outside play activities if you include these items in your children's ministry.
- ■ Set out simple games and puzzles if using the Welcome Time Activity.

 When you see this icon, it means preparation will take more than five minutes.

TICKETS PLEASE!
(Welcome and Bible Connection)

■ **Objective:** *To excite children's interest and connect their own life experiences with the Bible Truth, children will experience playing without seeing and talk about life as a blind person.*

Welcome Time Activity: Blind Experience

■ **Materials:** *blindfolds (optional), simple puzzles*

As children arrive, invite them to where you have simple puzzles laid out. Explain that they're going to try to play a game or put together a puzzle without using their eyes. Children can either close their eyes or be blindfolded. They can play/work alone or with a partner. As they try to do their activity choice, discuss with them other aspects of life that a blind person must experience.

Sharing Time and Bible Connection

Introduce today's lesson by discussing these questions with your students. As you talk, give every child the opportunity to say something.

■ **What would life be like if you couldn't see anything?**
■ **How do you think other people might treat someone who is blind?** (ignore them, make fun of them, try to help them)
■ **What other ways are people disabled or different from you and me?** (can't hear, missing limbs, crippled, mental disabilities, etc.)

After this sharing time, help your students connect their discussion to the Bible story they are about to hear from Matthew 20.

Life can be hard and lonely for people who are blind or have other disabilities. They can't do some things you and I enjoy, like riding a bike or watching a movie. They probably get left out of things or just ignored. <u>Jesus showed kindness</u> to many people who had disabilities. Let's see what example he left for us.

ALL ABOARD FOR BIBLE TRUTH

(Bible Discover and Learn Time)

Matthew 20:29-34

■ *Objective:* Children will study Matthew 20 to discover how Jesus showed kindness.
■ *Materials:* Bibles, pencils and paper

Break into three groups, with capable readers and writers in each group. Offer Bibles to children who don't have one. Direct children to find Matthew 20:29–34. Once everyone in the group has found the passage, one or two good readers can read the verses to their group. Each group should have one writer to scribe the group's ideas. On the whiteboard, show how to divide the paper into three columns. Instruct the groups to label each column with a person or group from the text: Jesus, two blind men, crowd. Under each heading, they should write what they observe about each person/group. When finished, come back together for groups to share their discoveries.

Now that you've seen for yourself how Jesus treated the two men who couldn't see, what have you learned? Help children summarize: **Jesus cared about the two men. <u>He showed kindness</u> to them. He didn't let the crowd keep him from showing kindness.**

Alternative: If time is limited, you can assign each group just one column of the chart instead of all three.

Use the Clues!
(Bible Review)

Okay, let's see what you remember. Show the Game Show Wheel. **Every week after our story we'll take turns spinning the Game Show Wheel. The color the wheel stops at shows what color question you'll answer. If you spin the "bonus" or "special" sections, you get to do something fun plus answer a question for double points.**

■ **Why did Jesus stop to talk to the two blind men?** (they asked for his help, they recognized he was the Son of God)

■ **What does the Bible say caused Jesus to help these men?** (he had compassion on them, he felt caring toward them)

■ **What does Jesus' example show us?** (we can show kindness to others, not to let what other people think keep us from being caring to those in need)

■ **We probably won't be able to make a blind person see. So how can we show kindness to others?** (pay attention to them, spend time with them, do what you can to help, be a friend, find out their needs and take care of a need)

■ **Who does the memory verse say we should be kind to?** (everyone)

■ (Review question) **What did a man healed from leprosy teach us last week?** (we should be ready to praise and thank Jesus for all he does for us)

Jesus didn't heal people to impress others. He wasn't showing off or making himself feel important. He expressed kindness because he cared about the people he met. <u>We can follow his example and show kindness to others too.</u>

BIBLE MEMORY WAYPOINT
(Scripture Memory)

1 Thessalonians 5:15

■ **Objective:** *Children will hide God's Word in their hearts for guidance, protection, and encouragement.*

■ **Materials:** *beanbag, numbered papers*

Read this week's memory verse from the poster. Point to each word as you read it:

Make sure that nobody pays back wrong for wrong, but **always try to be kind to each other and to everyone else (1 Thessalonians 5:15).**

To help children memorize the Bible verse, play a beanbag game. In an open area, randomly set out papers numbered from 3 to 24, by threes (3, 6, 9, 12, etc.). Mark a line to stand behind, then let children take turns standing with their back to the papers (so they can't see the numbers) and tossing a beanbag over their shoulder. Whatever number it lands on or closest to is the number of words of the verse they must repeat. Let them use the verse poster at first, but as the game progresses have them rely on their memory (and classmates' help).

PRAYER STATION

- **Objective:** *Children will explore and practice prayer for themselves in small groups.*
- **Materials:** *Copies of* StationMaster Card #5 *for each adult or teen helper*

Break into small groups of three to five children. Assign a teen or adult helper to each small group and give each helper a copy of *StationMaster Card #5* (see Resources) with ideas for group discussion and prayer.

SNACK STOP: CEREAL NECKLACES (Optional)

If you plan to provide a snack, this is an ideal time to serve it.

- **Materials:** *oaten-ring cereal, licorice strings or cloth string cut in 14" lengths*

Give children a handful of cereal and a licorice or cloth string. Challenge them to thread the cereal onto the string like a necklace—with their eyes closed. After they've mastered the challenge, talk with them as they eat about daily life with a disability like blindness or having only one hand or leg.

Note: Always be aware of children with food allergies and have another option on hand if necessary.

APPLICATION

- **Objective:** *Children will have opportunities to show how the lesson works in their own lives through activities and take-home papers.*

Some children's ministries may allow children to play outside at this point. If yours does not, choose one of the following activities.

Kindness Tag

Play the classic game of Freeze Tag. Once a player is tagged, the player freezes in place. Other players can show kindness by touching the frozen players and releasing them to play again. Make the game more challenging by having more than one "It."

 ## Kindness Bingo

■ *Materials: cardstock, thick markers, photocopied bingo images from page 84, glue sticks, scissors, small objects for bingo markers*

Make up bingo cards by using a thick marker to divide a sheet of cardstock into nine equal sections. Children will cut out the nine photocopied images and glue each in a section of their playing card. They may color the pictures if there's time. To play, children will color an image that resembles something they did during the coming week that is an act of kindness or mercy to a disabled person or someone else they know. The goal is to try to have three in a row (up/down, across, or diagonal) by next class time.

 ## ON THE FAST TRACK! *(Take-Home Papers)*

■ *Materials:* On the Fast Track! #5, *treasure box*

(Optional) Introduce the treasure box by asking: **Who would like to choose a prize from the treasure box?** Anticipate excited responses. Show *On the Fast Track!* take-home papers. **When you take this *On the Fast Track!* paper home each week and do the activities, your parents can sign the ticket that you finished the work. Bring the signed ticket back to choose a prize from the treasure box.** Distribute the take-home papers just before children leave.

Love God,
Not Things

Memory Verse:

Store up for yourselves treasures in heaven...for **where your treasure is, there your heart will be also (Matthew 6:20-21).**

*Note: Younger children may memorize the shorter version of this verse in **bold** print.*

Bible Basis:
Luke 12:15–21

Bible Truth:
Love God more than your stuff.

You Will Need:

- ☐ Game Show Wheel
- ☐ Game Show envelope board
- ☐ 1 poster board
- ☐ butcher paper
- ☐ markers or crayons
- ☐ tape
- ☐ beanbag or plush toy
- ☐ toy blocks
- ☐ Bibles
- ☐ *On the Fast Track! #6* take-home paper
- ☐ *StationMaster Card #6*
- ☐ (Optional) treasure box
- ☐ (Optional) snack: round crackers, cheese slices or bananas, plastic knife
- ☐ (Optional) Activity #1: small items like pennies, small blocks, construction-paper shapes, etc.
- ☐ (Optional) Activity #2: red cardstock with heart outline, pencils, scissors, envelopes

 When you see this icon, it means preparation will take more than five minutes.

 GET SET!
(Lesson Preparation)

- ■ Print today's Bible memory verse on a poster board: **Store up for yourselves treasures in heaven...for where your treasure is, there your heart will be also (Matthew 6:20–21).** Hang the poster board on the wall.
- ■ Copy *On the Fast Track #6* for each child.
- ■ Copy *StationMaster Card #6* for each helper.
- ■ Draw a large heart outline on red cardstock, one per child, if using Activity #2.
- ■ Set out the Game Show Wheel, Game Show envelope board, and (optional) treasure box.
- ■ Set up snack or outside play activities if you include these items in your children's ministry.
- ■ Mount a length of butcher paper at children's height on a wall and set markers nearby.

TICKETS PLEASE!
(Welcome and Bible Connection)

- ■ **Objective:** *To excite children's interest and connect their own life experiences with the Bible Truth, children will imagine having a lot of money and talk about what money can buy.*

Welcome Time Activity: "If I Had" Mural

■ *Materials: butcher paper, markers or crayons, tape*
  As children arrive, direct them to the wall where you have taped the butcher paper. Invite children to draw some of the things they would do or buy if they had $1,000. Comment on their works in progress and encourage them to share what their drawings show about what is important to them.

Sharing Time and Bible Connection

Introduce today's lesson by discussing these questions with your students. As you talk, give every child the opportunity to say something.

■ **What are some things you would do if you were given a handful of money?**
■ **How can having money make problems for people?** (can make them greedy, jealous, selfish, wanting more, trying to get lots of stuff)
■ **What kind of treasures do you think can be stored up in heaven?** (doing things for others, sharing what you have with those who have less, serving God)

After this sharing time, help your students connect their discussion to the Bible story they are about to hear from Luke 12.

Money is a good thing, but it can also be a problem. It can cause every one of us to get greedy and want more and more. It seems like the more stuff a person has, the more he wants. Jesus knows that money and the things we buy can get too important to us. That's why he told a parable about a rich man who forgot that we should <u>love God more than our stuff</u>.

ALL ABOARD FOR BIBLE TRUTH   Luke 12:15-21
(Bible Discover and Learn Time)

■ *Objective: Children will study Luke 12 and discover what treasure Jesus said is the most important.*
■ *Materials: toy blocks, Bibles*

As we read the story Jesus told in the book of Luke, we're all going to do what the man in the story did.

Hand out Bibles to confident readers and ask them to find Luke 12:15. Pass out enough blocks to each child (or pair up children to build together) to construct a small four-sided barn. Build one, or have a helper build one as an example.

When these first buildings are finished, ask a volunteer to read Luke 12:15–18. **The rich man had more crops than he needed, but he wanted to keep them all. So he took down his barns and built bigger ones. He wanted to have more and more stuff.** Guide children in toppling their small barns while you hand out more blocks. **Like the rich man in Jesus' story, let's build bigger barns to store all our stuff.**

When these barns are completed, ask another volunteer to read Luke 12:19. **Now that the rich man had all this stuff stored in his bigger barns, he felt secure and happy with himself. He had so much good stuff! So let's all relax and enjoy looking at our huge barns filled with things.** Stretch out on the floor with your hands behind your head and look pleased with yourself.

But having all that stuff didn't make the man a better follower of God, did it? It just made him rich. Was he sharing what he had to help those who didn't have as much? Was he giving some of his stuff for the work God wanted to do? (no) **All that stuff was nice, but it was really a trap. It made the man feel safe, but actually he was being very foolish.**

Ask a volunteer to read Luke 12:20. **What happened to the man who thought he had everything he wanted?** (he died and lost all he had accumulated) Have the kids knock down their barns. **Working hard to collect all the stuff so he could look at it and feel proud and safe was actually useless.** Read Luke 12:21. **What was the problem this rich man had?** (he had lots of stuff, but loved it more than he loved God; he had riches on earth, but nothing that counted in God's eyes)

If having lots of money and possessions doesn't make us rich in heaven, what does? (doing what pleases God, sharing what we have, giving to God's work, serving God, living God's way, showing love instead of being greedy and selfish) **God doesn't say money and things are bad. But our stuff can become so important to us that we forget what God made us for. Jesus taught us that to be rich in heaven means we need to** <u>love God more than our stuff</u>.

Use the Clues!
(Bible Review)

Okay, let's see what you remember. Show the Game Show Wheel. **Every week after our story we'll take turns spinning the Game Show Wheel. The color the wheel stops at shows what** color question you'll answer. If you spin the "bonus" or "special" sections, you get to do something fun plus answer a question for double points.

■ **How did the rich man use all his crops and money?** (he kept them for himself and made himself rich)

- **Why did Jesus call this rich man foolish?** (he let his stuff become more important than God, he didn't store up any treasures in heaven)
- **Why would Jesus want us to store up treasures in heaven rather than on earth?** (because things on earth will get old, used up, or lost, but what we do for God lasts forever)
- **How can you and I be rich toward God?** (do what pleases God, share what we have, give to God's work, serve God, live God's way, show love to others, love God more than our stuff)
- **What does the way we treat our stuff show about our hearts, according to the memory verse?** (the way we use our stuff shows what's most important to us)
- *(Review question)* **Tell one of the things you've learned in the past six weeks about what Jesus taught us.**

BIBLE MEMORY WAYPOINT   Matthew 6:20–21
(Scripture Memory)

- ***Objective:*** *Children will hide God's Word in their hearts for guidance, protection, and encouragement.*
- ***Materials:*** *beanbag or plush toy*

Read this week's memory verse from the poster. Point to each word as you read it:

Store up / for yourselves / treasures in heaven/ …for where your treasure is, / there your heart / will be also / (Matthew 6:20–21).

Help the children learn the verse by phrases. Add a slash mark (/) between short phrases as shown above. Then practice the verse with this game. Divide the class in half, with the groups lining up facing each other, children side by side. Toss a beanbag or plush toy to the first child on one side. He'll say the first phrase and toss the bag to the child across from him, who will say the second phrase, then toss the bag to the next child across from him, who recites the third phrase. Continue down the double line as the verse is recited all the way through. Start the verse again and continue, going back down the row as the recitation speeds up. Encourage the children to speak and toss quickly enough that the verse is recited smoothly.

PRAYER STATION

- **Objective:** *Children will explore and practice prayer for themselves in small groups.*
- **Materials:** *Copies of StationMaster Card #6 for each adult or teen helper*

Break into small groups of three to five children. Assign a teen or adult helper to each small group and give each helper a copy of *StationMaster Card #6* (see Resources) with ideas for group discussion and prayer.

SNACK STOP: TREASURE NIBBLES (Optional)

If you plan to provide a snack, this is an ideal time to serve it.

- **Materials:** *round crackers, cheese slices or bananas, plastic knife*

Serve round crackers. Cut cheese slices or slice bananas to fit the crackers. As children snack, talk about how our bodies know when we've had enough to eat. Ask: **How do we know when we have enough things?**

Note: Always be aware of children with food allergies and have another option on hand if necessary.

APPLICATION

- **Objective:** *Children will have opportunities to show how the lesson works in their own lives through activities and take-home papers.*

Some children's ministries may allow children to play outside at this point. If yours does not, choose one of the following activities.

Treasure Hunt

- ***Materials:*** *small items like pennies, small blocks, construction-paper shapes, etc.*

    Have the children go away from the play area or cover their eyes while you and helpers hide the small objects around the room. When all are hidden, let children search for them. When all have been found, ask the children to show what they discovered. Ask: **If this was treasure on earth, how could you use it for heavenly treasure?** (help support missionaries, put it in the offering, help needy people, etc.) Hide the items again and this time tell each child to collect only a small number of items (choose a small number based on your total number of items). After they've reached that amount, they should help others who haven't found as much to search.

 Heart Puzzle

- ***Materials:*** *red cardstock with heart outline, pencils, scissors, envelopes*

    Inside the heart outline, children will write, "My treasure is in heaven" (helpers write for young children). They can write in wavy lines, around the heart edge, or however they choose. Then have them draw lines that will be the puzzle-piece edges. Each puzzle should have four to eight pieces. Have children cut out their heart and then cut the puzzle lines to create a personal puzzle. Kids can try putting together each other's puzzles. Place pieces in envelopes to take home.

 ON THE FAST TRACK! *(Take-Home Papers)*

- ***Materials:*** On the Fast Track! #6, *treasure box*

(Optional) Introduce the treasure box by asking: **Who would like to choose a prize from the treasure box?** Anticipate excited responses. Show *On the Fast Track!* take-home papers. **When you take this *On the Fast Track!* paper home each week and do the activities, your parents can sign the ticket that you finished the work. Bring the signed ticket back to choose a prize from the treasure box.** Distribute the take-home papers just before children leave.

LESSON SEVEN: Jesus, the Healer

Memory Verse:

"The King will reply, 'I tell you the truth, **whatever you did for one of the least of these brothers of mine, you did for me'**" (Matthew 25:40).

*Note: Younger children may memorize the shorter version of this verse in **bold** print.*

Bible Basis:
John 5:2–9

Bible Truth:
Like Jesus, we can show mercy.

You Will Need:

- ☐ Game Show Wheel
- ☐ Game Show envelope board
- ☐ 1 poster board
- ☐ rolls of toilet paper
- ☐ large white sheet
- ☐ one or two spotlights or construction-type lights
- ☐ (Optional) cot
- ☐ On the Fast Track! #7 take-home paper
- ☐ StationMaster Card #7
- ☐ (Optional) treasure box
- ☐ (Optional) snack: small bear graham crackers, small cups of lemonade or white grape juice
- ☐ (Optional) Activity #1: large towels or sheets
- ☐ (Optional) Activity #2: undecorated, unwaxed cardboard cups, permanent markers

 GET SET!
(Lesson Preparation)

- ■ ⏱ Print today's Bible memory verse on a poster board: "**The King will reply, 'I tell you the truth, whatever you did for one of the least of these brothers of mine, you did for me'**" (Matthew 25:40). Hang the poster board on the wall.
- ■ Photocopy *On the Fast Track #7* for each child.
- ■ Photocopy *StationMaster Card #7* for each helper.
- ■ Set out the Game Show Wheel, Game Show envelope board, and *(optional)* treasure box.
- ■ ⏱ Set up the sheet and lights to produce a shadow play for the Bible story. Set up the sheet a few feet from the story area, with room behind it for the lights to cast a stark shadow against the back of the sheet. Place the cot, if using, to one side of the back of the sheet.
- ■ Set up snack or outside play activities if you include these items in your children's ministry.
- ■ Set out the toilet paper rolls if using the Welcome Time Activity.

 When you see this icon, it means preparation will take more than five minutes.

 # TICKETS PLEASE!
(Welcome and Bible Connection)

■ **Objective:** *To excite children's interest and connect their own life experiences with the Bible Truth, children will play a fun game and talk about what it means to show mercy.*

Welcome Time Activity: Medical Makeover

■ **Materials:** *rolls of toilet paper*

As children arrive, invite them to help "make over" another student by using a roll of paper to wrap the person, mummy style. (Noses, eyes, and mouths should not be covered.) Expect more than one child to want to be the "model" to get a makeover. After the fun is done, ask children what it means to show mercy.

Sharing Time and Bible Connection

Introduce today's lesson by discussing these questions with your students in the large group. As you talk, give every child the opportunity to say something.

■ **If you've ever had a broken foot or leg, what was it like?**
■ **Who helps you when you're sick or have a bad injury, like a broken leg or arm?**
(parents, family, doctors)
■ **What do you think life would be like if you couldn't walk at all for the rest of your life?**

After this sharing time, help your students connect their discussion to the Bible story they are about to hear from John 5:

Today we have many ways to get better when we're sick or hurt. When Jesus lived thousands of years ago, many people never got better when they were sick or hurt. And people didn't care much about those who needed help. In today's Bible story, you'll find out how Jesus showed mercy when no one else cared about a man.

ALL ABOARD FOR BIBLE TRUTH

John 5:2-9

(Bible Discover and Learn Time)

- **Objective:** *Children will study John 5 and understand how Jesus showed mercy to a man who couldn't walk.*
- **Materials:** *large white sheet, one or two spotlights or construction-type lights, cot (optional)*

Set up the sheet a few feet from the story area, with room behind it for the lights to cast a stark shadow against the back of the sheet. The children will face the sheet to watch a shadow enactment as you read the Scripture passage. Ask two helpers to act the parts of the lame man and Jesus behind the sheet. The lame man should lie on the floor or on a cot. Jesus will enter the tableau at the appropriate part in the reading. The lame man should groan and call out "Help me" occasionally, until Jesus comes in.

Read John 5:1–17 in a child-friendly Bible translation. Ask two other male helpers or adults to read the quotes of the sick man and Jesus.

The man who couldn't walk for 38 years had no one to help him. But Jesus did. Jesus made a difference in that man's life. We can make a difference in people's lives too, by helping with whatever ability we have. <u>God is pleased when we show mercy the way Jesus did</u>.

Use the Clues!

(Bible Review)

Okay, let's see what you remember. Show the Game Show Wheel. **Every week after our story we'll take turns spinning the Game Show Wheel. The color the wheel stops at shows what color question you'll answer. If you spin the "bonus" or "special" sections, you get to do something fun plus answer a question for double points.**

- **What was the problem of the man by the pool?** (he was lame, couldn't walk, he had been sick 38 years, he wanted to get into a pool of water that might help him feel better)
- **How did Jesus show mercy to the lame man?** (he noticed the man, he made him well)
- **Why did Jesus choose to show mercy to this man?** (Jesus could see his need, Jesus cared about the man, he saw something he could do and did it)
- **How can we show mercy to people we see who are in need?** (spend time with them, find out what they need and see if we

can help, share our extra blankets and food with the hungry, etc.)

■ **What does the memory verse say about caring for someone in need?** (caring for the least of people is the same as showing care for God)

■ *(Review question)* **What did Jesus teach us about storing up treasures?** (to do things that are treasures for heaven, like serving God and others, instead of accumulating stuff, to love God more than our stuff)

BIBLE MEMORY WAYPOINT   Matthew 25:40
(Scripture Memory)

■ *Objective: Children will hide God's Word in their hearts for guidance, protection, and encouragement.*

Read this week's memory verse from the poster. Point to each word as you read it:

"The King will reply, 'I tell you the truth, whatever you did for one of the least of these brothers of mine, you did for me' " (Matthew 25:40).

To help children memorize the Bible verse, call out categories. Whoever fits that category repeats the verse in unison. Categories can be girls/boys, color of hair, age, color of shirt or dress, or birthday months.

PRAYER STATION

■ *Objective: Children will explore and practice prayer for themselves in small groups.*
■ *Materials: Copies of* StationMaster Card #7 *for each adult or teen helper*

Break into small groups of three to five children. Assign a teen or adult helper to each small group and give each helper a copy of *StationMaster Card #7* (see Resources) with ideas for group discussion and prayer.

SNACK STOP: DUNKING BEARS (Optional)

If you plan to provide a snack, this is an ideal time to serve it.

■ *Materials: small bear graham crackers, small cups of lemonade or white grape juice*

Ask children to retell the main points of the story. Explain how people at the pool where the man was lying believed that at certain times the water in the pool would be stirred up and whoever got into the water first could be healed of their sickness. Kids can dunk their bear crackers in their juice like the people going into the water. After eating, pray briefly to thank Jesus for the mercy he shows us.

Note: Always be aware of children with food allergies and have another option on hand if necessary.

 ## APPLICATION

■ *Objective: Children will have opportunities to show how the lesson works in their own lives through activities and take-home papers.*

Some children's ministries may allow children to play outside at this point. If yours does not, choose one of the following activities.

Foot-free Race

■ *Materials: large towels or sheets*

Divide into two teams. Form a large circle, with each team as one half of the circle. Hand the first two players from each team (opposite side of circle from each other) a towel or sheet. The third player in line will sit or lie on the towel as the other two drag it around the outside of the circle, returning to their spot. They'll hand off the towel to the next couple of teammates to pull another player around. Continue until all players on each team have participated.

 Cup of Mercy

■ *Materials: undecorated, unwaxed cardboard cups, permanent markers*

Ask children for their thoughts on ways to show mercy. Explain that being merciful can be as easy as seeing someone who is hot and thirsty and offering her a cup of cool water. It's showing care for someone in need. Children can write/draw encouraging words and pictures on their cups, including words about Jesus (Jesus cares about you, Trust in Jesus). Send the cups home with children, suggesting they ask God to point them in the direction of someone who is in need of mercy this week.

 ON THE FAST TRACK! *(Take-Home Papers)*

■ *Materials:* On the Fast Track! #7, *treasure box*

(Optional) Introduce the treasure box by asking: **Who would like to choose a prize from the treasure box?** Anticipate excited responses. Show *On the Fast Track!* take-home papers. **When you take this *On the Fast Track!* paper home each week and do the activities, your parents can sign the ticket that you finished the work. Bring the signed ticket back to choose a prize from the treasure box.** Distribute the take-home papers just before children leave.

LESSON EIGHT: Jesus' New Commandments

Memory Verse:

He answered: " 'Love the Lord your God with all **your heart and** with all your **soul and** with all your **strength and** with all your **mind'; and 'Love your neighbor as yourself' "** (Luke 10:27).

*Note: Younger children may memorize the shorter version of this verse in **bold** print.*

Bible Basis:

Matthew 22:35–40

Bible Truth:

Love Jesus first, and others next.

You Will Need:

- ☐ Game Show Wheel
- ☐ Game Show envelope board
- ☐ play dough
- ☐ poster boards
- ☐ markers
- ☐ glue
- ☐ scissors
- ☐ art supplies (glitter glue, sequins, felt, yarn, buttons, puff paint, chenille stems, etc.)
- ☐ Bibles
- ☐ *On the Fast Track! #8* take-home paper
- ☐ *StationMaster Card #8*
- ☐ *(Optional)* treasure box
- ☐ *(Optional)* snack: sugar cookies, icing in squeeze dispensers
- ☐ *(Optional)* Activity #1: inflated balloons containing real-life situations
- ☐ *(Optional)* Activity #2: brown-paper lunch sacks, raffia or yarn, scissors, stickers, glitter glue

 When you see this icon, it means preparation will take more than five minutes.

GET SET!
(Lesson Preparation)

- ■ 🕐 Print today's Bible memory verse on poster board: **He answered: ""Love the Lord your God with all your heart and with all your soul and with all your strength and with all your mind'; and 'Love your neighbor as yourself' "** (Luke 10:27). Hang the poster on the wall.
- ■ Photocopy *On the Fast Track #8* for each child.
- ■ Photocopy *StationMaster Card #8* for each helper.
- ■ Set out the Game Show Wheel, Game Show envelope board, and *(optional)* treasure box.
- ■ Set up snack or outside play activities if you include these items in your children's ministry.
- ■ 🕐 If using Activity #1, print situations that call for acts of love, like comforting a hurting friend, on slips of paper and insert in balloons. Blow up and tie the balloons.
- ■ Set out play dough at the Welcome Time Activity table, if using.

TICKETS PLEASE!
(Welcome and Bible Connection)

■ *Objective:* To excite children's interest and connect their own life experiences with the Bible Truth, children will make play-dough figures and talk about things they love most.

Welcome Time Activity: Top 5

■ *Materials:* play dough

As children arrive, direct them to tables where play dough awaits. Invite them to create up to five things they love most. When done, ask kids to share what they've made with the other children.

Sharing Time and Bible Connection

Introduce today's lesson by discussing these questions with children. As you talk, give every child the opportunity to say something.

■ **What are some things you love a lot?**
■ **How do you show your love to people who are important to you?**

After this sharing time, help your students connect their discussion to the Bible story they are about to hear from Matthew 22.

Do you remember how many commandments God gave the Israelites in the Old Testament? (10) **When Jesus came to live on earth, he said there were two greatest commandments. Let's see what Jesus said about these two commandments.**

ALL ABOARD FOR BIBLE TRUTH   Matthew 22:35–40
(Bible Discover and Learn Time)

■ *Objective:* Children will study Matthew 22 and hear what Jesus said are the two most important commandments.
■ *Materials:* poster board, markers, glue, scissors, miscellaneous art supplies (glitter glue, sequins, felt, yarn, buttons, puff paint, chenille stems, etc.), Bibles

Tell the children they'll be making posters of the Bible story. Break the class into groups of three to five students and divide the art supplies among the groups. Guide students to find Matthew 22:35–40. A confident reader in each group can read the verses out loud.

On your group poster board, you can use the art supplies in the way you want in order to show the two commandments Jesus gives in Matthew 22:35–40. Allow the children time to create their visual display of the Bible text. Give groups time to share their posters with the other groups, then mount the posters in the room.

Jesus said if we love him, we'll do what he commands. And even though <u>loving God best and loving others second</u> are simple commandments, living by them every day isn't that easy. It's natural for us to want to think of ourselves first. But like tying your shoes or learning to skateboard, the more you put God and others first, the easier it gets.

Use the Clues!
(Bible Review)

Okay, let's see what you remember. Show the Game Show Wheel. **Every week after our story we'll take turns spinning the Game Show Wheel. The color the wheel stops at shows what color question you'll answer. If you spin the "bonus" or "special" sections, you get to do something fun plus answer a question for double points.**

■ **What did Jesus say was the greatest commandment?** (love God with all your heart, soul, strength, and mind)

■ **And what was the next-greatest commandment?** (love others as you do yourself)

■ **How do we show God we love him the best?** (talk to him often, obey him, read his Word, do the things that please him)

■ **How will others know we love them?** (by the way we treat them, choosing to give to and help them, thinking of them as often as we think of our own cares, sharing our things with them)

■ **Do you think we don't need the Ten Commandments anymore, since we have these two new ones?** (if we follow the two commands Jesus said, we will also be following the Ten Commandments; everything in the 10 is part of the two)

■ *(Review question)* **What does it mean to show mercy?** (to help those in need and care for them no matter who they are or what they need)

BIBLE MEMORY WAYPOINT
(Scripture Memory)

Luke 10:27

■ **Objective:** *Children will hide God's Word in their hearts for guidance, protection, and encouragement.*

Read this week's memory verse from the poster board. Point to each word as you read it:

He answered: " 'Love the Lord your God with all your heart and with all your soul and with all your strength and with all your mind'; and 'Love your neighbor as yourself' " (Luke 10:27).

To practice the verse, have your snack time now (see Snack Stop). Once the children have all their cookies ready, have them get groups of two to four kids and practice the verse. As they say the first part, **"He answered: 'Love the Lord your God with all your heart and with all your soul and with all your strength and with all your mind'"** they'll hold up the "1" cookie, then hold up the "2" cookie as they say the second part of the verse. This can also be done as a chant bouncing between two children: One child holds up the "1" and says that part of the verse, then the partner finishes the verse with the "2" cookie.

PRAYER STATION

■ **Objective:** *Children will explore and practice prayer for themselves in small groups.*
■ **Materials:** *Copies of* StationMaster Card #8 *for each adult or teen helper*

Break into small groups of three to five children. Assign a teen or adult helper to each small group and give each helper a copy of *StationMaster Card #8* (see Resources) with ideas for group discussion and prayer.

SNACK STOP: COMMANDMENT COOKIES (Optional)

If you plan to provide a snack, this is an ideal time to serve it.

■ *Materials: sugar cookies, icing in squeezable dispensers*

Note: This portion of the class time can be used earlier in the lesson for the Bible Memory activity, or used in the typical way. Offer each child two cookies. Show them how to squeeze out the icing to write a "1" on one cookie, and a "2" on the other. Relate these numbers to the two commandments Jesus taught.

   Note: Always be aware of children with food allergies and have another option on hand if necessary.

APPLICATION

■ *Objective: Children will have opportunities to show how the lesson works in their own lives through activities and take-home papers.*

Some children's ministries may allow children to play outside at this point. If yours does not, choose one of the following activities.

Pop a Question

■ *Materials: inflated balloons containing real-life situations*

We can say we love Jesus and others, but until we act in love, our ideas are just air. Inside each balloon is a situation that calls for love. Children will pair up and take turns with their partner trying to pop a balloon by sitting on it. Once popped they'll read the piece of paper inside, or have a helper read it to them, then make up a simple skit showing the situation and how to live out Jesus' two commandments. Pairs will perform after every pair has popped a balloon and received a situation slip.

Love Bags

■ *Materials: brown-paper lunch sacks, raffia or yarn, scissors, stickers, glitter glue*

Ask children to call out people who Jesus might want them to show love to this week. Encourage them to think beyond family and familiar friends; consider a homeless child on the street, an elderly person in a nursing home, a shut-in in their neighborhood, a recent widow/widower, etc. Have them decorate one or more bags to serve as Love Bags. They'll take home the bag (tuck raffia or yarn tie closure inside) to fill with things like pocket tissues, a decorated Bible verse card, hard candies, a crossword puzzle, a small gift card for an ice cream or sandwich from a local eatery, etc.

ON THE FAST TRACK! *(Take-Home Papers)*

■ *Materials:* On the Fast Track! #8, *treasure box*

(Optional) Introduce the treasure box by asking: **Who would like to choose a prize from the treasure box?** Anticipate excited responses. Show *On the Fast Track!* **take-home papers. When you take this *On the Fast Track!* paper home each week and do the activities, your parents can sign the ticket that you finished the work. Bring the signed ticket back to choose a prize from the treasure box.** Distribute the take-home papers just before children leave.

LESSON NINE: Jesus Deserves Honor

Honor Jesus

Memory Verse:

You are worthy, our Lord and God, to receive glory and honor and power, for you created all things, and by your will they were created and have their being **(Revelation 4:11)**.

*Note: Younger children may memorize the shorter version of this verse in **bold** print.*

Bible Basis:
John 12:1–8

Bible Truth:
Let's honor Jesus with our best.

You Will Need:

- [ ] Game Show Wheel
- [ ] Game Show envelope board
- [ ] 1 poster board
- [ ] paper cups
- [ ] small empty boxes
- [ ] cardboard tubes
- [ ] paper plates
- [ ] small balls (golf, foam)
- [ ] tape
- [ ] glue sticks
- [ ] perfume in fancy bottle
- [ ] fancy place setting: plate, place mat, fabric napkin, napkin ring, silver utensils, stemmed glass bottle (fancy if possible) of perfume, vase with flower, small cloth bag of coins
- [ ] *On the Fast Track! #9* take-home paper
- [ ] *StationMaster Card #9*
- [ ] *(Optional)* treasure box
- [ ] *(Optional)* snack: mini-bagel halves, whipped cream cheese tinted yellow, or lemon-flavored frosting, cheese puffs, plastic knives
- [ ] *(Optional)* Activity #1: one set per team of plastic/casual dinnerware (cup, plate, saucer, bowl, utensils, napkin, place mat)
- [ ] *(Optional)* Activity #2: construction paper, markers, butcher paper, scissors, glue sticks

 When you see this icon, it means preparation will take more than five minutes.

GET SET!
(Lesson Preparation)

- ▪ Print today's Bible memory verse on a poster board: **You are worthy, our Lord and God, to receive glory and honor and power, for you created all things, and by your will they were created and have their being (Revelation 4:11)**. Hang the poster board on the wall.
- ▪ Photocopy *On the Fast Track #9* for each child.
- ▪ Photocopy *StationMaster Card #9* for each helper.
- ▪ Set out the Game Show Wheel, Game Show envelope board, and *(optional)* treasure box.
- ▪ Set up snack or outside play activities if you include these items in your children's ministry.
- ▪ Set out paper cups, plates, cardboard tubes, balls, boxes, tape, and glue sticks on tables for the Welcome Time Activity if using.

TICKETS PLEASE!
(Welcome and Bible Connection)

- ▪ **Objective:** *To excite children's interest and connect their own life experiences with the Bible Truth, children will create trophies from recycled materials and talk about what it means to honor someone.*

Welcome Time Activity: Trophy Design Center

■ *Materials: paper cups, small empty boxes, cardboard tubes, paper plates, small balls (golf, foam), tape, glue sticks*

As children arrive, direct them to a table where the assorted supplies await. Tell them they can create a trophy using the materials. Children can work together or independently. While working, engage the children in conversation about what trophies are given for and what they represent (honor for some achievement or status).

Sharing Time and Bible Connection

Introduce today's lesson by discussing these questions with children. As you talk, give every child the opportunity to say something.

■ **Who can you think of that is someone we show honor to?** (President, heroes, Olympic medal winners, firemen, and policemen)
■ **How do you show honor to someone?** (respectful greetings, giving them a medal or presenting them with something special, a ceremony)
■ **How would you honor a very special guest in your home?** (clean up the house, give them a present, make a great dinner for them)

After this sharing time, help your students connect their discussion to the Bible story they are about to hear from John 12.

Has anyone here had a president or hero come to your house for dinner? Wait for show of hands. **We think about famous people when we talk about honoring someone. In today's Bible story, a lady was expecting a special guest at her house. She showed this person great honor. Let's find out what she did.**

ALL ABOARD FOR BIBLE TRUTH

John 12:1-8

(Bible Discover and Learn Time)

■ **Objective:** *Children will study John 12 to find out how Jesus was honored by a woman.*
■ **Materials:** *bottle (fancy if possible) of perfume, beautiful place setting (place mat, plate, cloth napkin in napkin ring, silver utensils, stemmed drinking glass, vase with flower, small cloth bag of coins)*

As children watch, put out the place setting with care. Lay the perfume bottle and bag of money next to it.

As you arrange the place setting, ask: **What do think this is for?** (getting ready for a meal) **This is my best set of dishes and my nicest napkin and place mat. When have you seen someone use his best dishes and things at home**? (for special guests, a special event)

How would your family prepare for a dinner if the president was coming? (clean the house well, make special food, use the best dishes) **Imagine that this table is being set for the most important guest. What else would you do to show the guest of honor how pleased you were to have him or her with you?** Accept responses.

Our Bible story today is about a woman who was expecting someone she wanted to honor. Her name was Mary. This isn't Mary, Jesus' mother. It's a different Mary. She was expecting Jesus to come to her house for dinner. He was traveling through her town of Bethany on the way to Jerusalem. So she was preparing and working, along with her sister Martha, to honor him.

They ate dinner and then sat and talked. Besides the sisters Mary and Martha, their brother was with them. Do you recognize the name Lazarus? Jesus had brought him back to life after he died from a sickness. So you can see how precious Jesus was to this family. He had given their brother back to them.

After dinner, Mary did something very unusual. Pick up the perfume bottle. **She took a pound of very expensive perfume. It was a beautiful-smelling perfume from a faraway country.** Pass around or have a helper carry around the perfume so children can smell if they choose. **It would probably have cost a year's worth of work to buy. It was such a valuable perfume. It was used to anoint or pour over a king to honor him. Mary poured the whole jar over Jesus' feet. Then she wiped his feet with her hair. Oh, can you imagine how good their house smelled as the perfume's fragrance drifted in the air?**

It sounds like a strange way to use perfume. To Mary, it made perfect sense. She loved Jesus and knew he was God's Son. She wanted to show her honor for him in a meaningful way. She used an expensive treasure to show Jesus she believed he was the Savior.

Judas, one of Jesus' disciples, was at the dinner table too. He complained about how much money Mary was wasting by pouring it on Jesus. "She could have sold that perfume and given the money to poor people," he grumbled. But Jesus saw into Mary's heart. He understood that she was giving him a special gift of honor.

You and I don't have a chance to do something like that for Jesus to show him that we honor him. We honor him when we give him our best: our best time, our best efforts in school and at home, the first of our money, and the best part of our hearts. <u>Jesus is always honored when we give him our best</u>, whatever it is.

Use the Clues!
(Bible Review)

Okay, let's see what you remember. Show the Game Show Wheel. **Every week after our story we'll take turns spinning the Game Show Wheel. The color the wheel stops at shows what color question you'll answer. If you spin the "bonus" or "special" sections, you get to do something fun plus answer a question for double points.**

- **Who had Jesus come for dinner in Bethany?** (Mary, Martha, and Lazarus)
- **Why did Mary pour her expensive perfume on Jesus?** (to show him honor, as a way of showing her love and respect for him)
- **Was Judas right in complaining about such a waste of money?** (no, Jesus understood Mary's desire to honor him)
- **How could you and I show honor to Jesus?** (by giving our tithes and offerings cheerfully, working at whatever we do with our best efforts)
- **What does our memory verse say about honoring God?** (we should honor him because he created everything and keeps it all alive, he is worthy of all the glory and honor and power)
- *(Review question)* **What did Jesus say are the two commandments we need to live by?** (love God first and others second)

BIBLE MEMORY WAYPOINT
(Scripture Memory)

Revelation 4:11

- ***Objective:*** *Children will hide God's Word in their hearts for guidance, protection, and encouragement.*

Read this week's memory verse from the poster. Point to each word as you read it:

You are worthy, our Lord and God, to receive glory and honor and power, for you created all things, and by your will they were created and have their being (Revelation 4:11).

Help the class memorize the verse by using rhythm and clapping. Work with phrases of the verse. Say "you are worthy" followed by three sharp claps, which the class should echo back to you. Do the same with the next phrases, breaking them into rhythmic chunks. As you add more segments each time, keep saying the previous portions.

PRAYER STATION

- **Objective:** *Children will explore and practice prayer for themselves in small groups.*
- **Materials:** *Copies of* StationMaster Card #9 *for each adult or teen helper*

Break into small groups of three to five children. Assign a teen or adult helper to each small group and give each helper a copy of *StationMaster Card #9* (see Resources) with ideas for group discussion and prayer.

SNACK STOP: SHINING GLORY (Optional)

If you plan to provide a snack, this is an ideal time to serve it.

- **Materials:** *mini-bagel halves, whipped cream cheese tinted yellow or lemon-flavored frosting, cheese puffs, plastic knives*

The Bible says God's glory is brighter than the sun. When you see the sun, you can be reminded to honor God and his Son, Jesus, by giving your best. Explain how to make a sun snack: spread yellow cream cheese or frosting on a bagel half, then surround with cheese puff "rays."

Note: Always be aware of children with food allergies and have another option on hand if necessary.

APPLICATION

- **Objective:** *Children will have opportunities to show how the lesson works in their own lives through activities and take-home papers.*

Some children's ministries may allow children to play outside at this point. If yours does not, choose one of the following activities.

Set the Table Relay

■ *Materials: one set per team of plastic/casual dinnerware (cup, plate, saucer, bowl, utensils, napkin, place mat)*

Form two or more teams, each lined up front to back. In front of the starting players, lay one set of dinnerware (one set per team). At the opposite end of the room have a table or tape an "X" on the floor. On your signal, each starting player takes one item and passes it between his legs to the next player, until it has traveled between all the players' legs. The last player in line runs to the table/"X," lays down the item, then races to the front of the line and sends down the next item. A team wins when their place setting is set in an approximation of how it should look at a dinner table. Consider placing older players at the end of each team, so they can rearrange the place setting as needed.

Honor Collage

■ *Materials: construction paper, markers, butcher paper, scissors, glue sticks*

Ask children to create an Honor Collage with ways they can honor God. Pass out construction paper and markers so students can draw ways they can honor the Lord. They might draw things like worshipping him, giving offerings, helping someone, or trying your hardest at school so your work honors God. After they finish their drawings, have them cut them out using fun shapes like hearts, diamonds, and circles, and then glue them to the butcher paper to make a collage you can post in the class.

ON THE FAST TRACK! *(Take-Home Papers)*

■ *Materials:* On the Fast Track! #9, *treasure box*

(Optional) Introduce the treasure box by asking: **Who would like to choose a prize from the treasure box?** Anticipate excited responses. Show *On the Fast Track!* take-home papers. **When you take this *On the Fast Track!* paper home each week and do the activities, your parents can sign the ticket that you finished the work. Bring the signed ticket back to choose a prize from the treasure box.** Distribute the take-home papers just before children leave.

Memory Verse:
The Word became flesh and made his dwelling among us. We have seen his glory, the glory of the One and Only, who came from the Father, full of grace and truth **(John 1:14).**
*Note: Younger children may memorize the shorter version of this verse in **bold** print.*

Bible Basis:
Luke 22:7–20

Bible Truth:
We remember what Jesus did for us.

You Will Need:
- ☐ Game Show Wheel
- ☐ Game Show envelope board
- ☐ cardstock, pencils, markers, scissors
- ☐ 1 poster board
- ☐ large matzo cracker or flat bread (such as pita bread)
- ☐ pottery or ceramic cup
- ☐ grape juice
- ☐ small paper cups
- ☐ floor pillows or couch cushions
- ☐ index cards
- ☐ *On the Fast Track! #10* take-home paper
- ☐ *StationMaster Card #10*
- ☐ (Optional) treasure box
- ☐ (Optional) snack: fig cookies, olives, cheese, matzo crackers, grape juice
- ☐ (Optional) Activity #1: (for each team) a washed carrot, slice of buttered bread, piece of cheese or ready-to-eat hot dog, half an apple, glass of juice or water, cookie or graham cracker, table and chairs
- ☐ (Optional) Activity #2: beads, jewelry cording, letter beads to spell Jesus

When you see this icon, it means preparation will take more than five minutes.

GET SET!
(Lesson Preparation)

- ■ ⏱ Print today's Bible memory verse on a poster board: **The Word became flesh and made his dwelling among us. We have seen his glory, the glory of the One and Only, who came from the Father, full of grace and truth (John 1:14).** Hang the poster board on the wall at the front of the classroom.
- ■ ⏱ Set up table with cushions for use during Bible Truth.
- ■ Photocopy *On the Fast Track #10* for each child.
- ■ Photocopy *StationMaster Card #10* for each helper.
- ■ Set out the Game Show Wheel, Game Show envelope board, and (optional) treasure box.
- ■ Set up snack or outside play activities if you include these items in your children's ministry.
- ■ ⏱ Write Bible verse on index cards, one word per card, for use in Bible Memory Waypoint.

TICKETS PLEASE!
(Welcome and Bible Connection)

- ■ **Objective:** *To excite children's interest and connect their own life experiences with the Bible Truth, children will make a framed picture and talk about how they remember special people.*

Welcome Time Activity: Framed

■ *Materials: cardstock, markers, pencils, scissors*
As children arrive, direct them to the table where supplies are set out. Helpers can invite children to draw a picture frame and inside it, draw a picture of someone they want to remember, like a grandparent who lives far away, a friend who has moved, a pet, etc. As they work, talk with them about other ways they remember people who are special to them.

Sharing Time and Bible Connection

Introduce today's lesson by discussing these questions with the group. As you talk, give every child the opportunity to say something.

■ **What are some special meals you have at your house on holidays?**
■ **What kinds of traditions do you have at holiday meals?** (saying thank you to God for the food, using special dishes, lighting candles, etc.)
■ **What helps you remember the traditions for holiday celebrations?** (parents talk about the traditions, look at photo albums)

After this sharing time, help your students connect their discussion to the Bible story they are about to hear from Luke 22.

Before he died on the cross, Jesus started a very special tradition. He taught his closest friends how to celebrate this tradition and what it meant so they could remember what Jesus was about to do. We celebrate the same tradition <u>to remember how Jesus died for us</u>.

ALL ABOARD FOR BIBLE TRUTH   Luke 22:7–20
(Bible Discover and Learn Time)

■ *Objective: Children will study Luke 22 and learn how Jesus shared the Last Supper with his disciples and left a tangible reminder of his sacrifice.*
■ *Materials: large matzo cracker or flat bread (such as pita bread), pottery or ceramic cup, grape juice, small paper cups, floor pillows or couch cushions*

Share the Bible story as you dramatize with the children the Last Supper. If possible, fold up legs of one or more large tables so they sit flat on the floor. Spread pillows or cushions around the tables so children can recline around the tables. Place a small paper cup at each child's place. Set the pottery cup of juice and bread/crackers at your place at the head of the table.

We're going to pretend we're at the last Passover meal Jesus shared with his disciples. We call this the Last Supper because it was Jesus' last meal before he died. It was a very important dinner.

The Jewish people celebrated Passover every year to remind themselves how God saved their people from the Egyptians by sending an angel of death. The first son of every Egyptian family was killed by God's angel, but the angel passed over every Jewish house that had a special mark on it. When the Jews celebrate Passover, they remember how God saved them. They have special foods at the dinner. A bread without yeast, like this matzo cracker, and wine are two things at their Passover meal. We'll pretend this grape juice is wine.

I'll pretend to be Jesus. You can pretend to be his disciples. How many were there? (12) In Jesus' time, people sort of lay around the table to eat. They didn't sit in chairs. So let's recline around the table. Show children how to lie back on the pillow, supporting yourself with one elbow. Children can try that or sit cross-legged if they choose.

Jesus told the disciples, "I've been looking forward to eating this Passover meal with you. I have important things I want you to understand before I leave you. Do all of you know how this meal was arranged for you?" Let children answer.

"This morning I sent Peter and John into the city. I told them they would see a man walking near the city gate carrying a jar of water. They were to follow him to a certain house and to ask the owner of the house if the Teacher could use his guest room to eat the Passover. This man let us use this room for our Passover meal."

Jesus told his disciples, his closest friends, to believe that he loved them no matter what they would do or think. He said, "There's nothing in the world that can change my love for you. I want you to remember this. Love one another because I love you. Serve each other. The best leader is one who looks for ways to serve."

Pick up the bread. **Jesus first thanked God for the food.** Bow your head and say a simple sentence prayer of thanks. **Then he broke the bread into pieces and passed it around to his friends.** Do this. **He told them, "This bread is like my body. It's broken and given for you; whenever you meet together to break bread in this way, do this in remembrance of me."** Eat your piece of bread and have children do the same. **Jesus was showing us that his body would be hurt to pay for our sins.**

Hold up the cup of juice. **Jesus said, "This cup is the new covenant in my blood, which is poured out for you."** Walk around the table and pour a small amount of juice in each child's cup. **Jesus wants us to remember how he suffered and died so his blood would count as the payment for what we've done wrong.**

He told the disciples, "I know you don't understand this now. Later I want you to remember this night and my words. This is how you can remember my sacrifice for you."

Drink from the cup and have children drink their juice.

This wasn't just a dinner. It was a very special event. We still remember this Last Supper when we have Communion (insert your church's term for the sacrament). **It's a very important and serious time to remember.**

The Last Supper was a gift Jesus left for us. Every time we do this together, <u>we remember how Jesus loved us and was willing to die in our place</u>. The bread and juice remind us of Jesus' body and blood.

Use the Clues!
(Bible Review)

Okay, let's see what you remember. Show the Game Show Wheel. **Every week after our story we'll take turns spinning the Game Show Wheel. The color the wheel stops at shows what color question you'll answer. If you spin the "bonus" or "special" sections, you get to do something fun plus answer a question for double points.**

- **What was the Passover about?** (remembering how God rescued the Jews from the Egyptians, how his angel of death passed over their homes)

- **What did Jesus say the bread reminds us of?** (his body, how his body was broken for us)
- **What is the cup to remind us of?** (Jesus' blood that paid for our sins)
- **Why do we still have the Last Supper?** (Jesus told us to do it to remember how he died for us)
- **What does the memory verse say about who Jesus is?** (he is a man who lived among us, he is full of glory, God's only Son, full of grace and truth)
- *(Review question)* **How do we show honor to Jesus?** (spending time with God, by giving our tithes and offerings cheerfully, working at whatever we do with our best efforts)

BIBLE MEMORY WAYPOINT
(Scripture Memory)

John 1:14

- *Objective: Children will hide God's Word in their hearts for guidance, protection, and encouragement.*
- *Materials: Bible verse written on index cards, one word per card, mixed up in order*

Read this week's memory verse from the poster. Point to each word as you read it:

The Word became flesh and made his dwelling among us. We have seen his glory, the glory of the One and Only, who came from the Father, full of grace and truth (John 1:14).

To help children memorize the verse, have them unscramble the mixed-up cards and then chant the verse together. Then hand out the cards to individual children. Have them arrange themselves in correct order. Once they are in order, they can pop up shouting their word to recite the verse. Repeat as needed so each child has a turn to participate.

PRAYER STATION

- **Objective:** *Children will explore and practice prayer for themselves in small groups.*
- **Materials:** *Copies of* StationMaster Card #10 *for each adult or teen helper*

Break into small groups of three to five children. Assign a teen or adult helper to each small group and give each helper a copy of *StationMaster Card #10* (see Resources) with ideas for group discussion and prayer.

SNACK STOP: PASSOVER SNACK (Optional)

If you plan to provide a snack, this is an ideal time to serve it.

- **Materials:** *fig cookies, olives, cheese slices, matzo crackers, grape juice*

Discuss the other items that may have been eaten as part of the meal. Then have the children retell the story using the crackers and juice. Ask: **What do the bread and wine stand for?**

Note: Always be aware of children with food allergies and have another option on hand if necessary.

APPLICATION

- **Objective:** *Children will have opportunities to show how the lesson works in their own lives through activities and take-home papers.*

Some children's ministries may allow children to play outside at this point. If yours does

Eat-Your-Supper Relay

■ *Materials: (for each team) a washed carrot, slice of buttered bread, piece of cheese or ready-to-eat hot dog, half an apple, glass of juice or water, cookie or graham cracker, table and chairs*

Divide into teams of six players per team. Place the food items on a table at the far end of the play area, with teams lined up at the opposite end. At "go," the first player will race to the table and sit down at his team's plate. The player must completely chew and swallow one item before getting up to race back so the next team member can go. Teams must eat the items in the order you designate.

 Remember Jesus

■ *Materials: beads, jewelry cording, letter beads to spell Jesus*

As another reminder of Jesus, children can string beads on a cord as a bracelet or anklet. If desired, they can also spell out J-E-S-U-S on their piece of jewelry. Once the beaded strand is finished, help each child tie on their bracelet or anklet if they wish, or they may use it as a bookmark. As the craft is worked on, discuss ways people remember others (scrapbooks, photo albums, framed photos, lockets, etc.).

not, choose one of the following activities.

 ON THE FAST TRACK! *(Take-Home Papers)*

■ *Materials:* On the Fast Track! #10, *treasure box*

(Optional) Introduce the treasure box by asking: **Who would like to choose a prize from the treasure box?** Anticipate excited responses. Show *On the Fast Track!* take-home papers. **When you take this *On the Fast Track!* paper home each week and do the activities, your parents can sign the ticket that you finished the work. Bring the signed ticket back to choose a prize from the treasure box.** Distribute the take-home papers just before children leave.

Jesus Loves So Much

Memory Verse:

Jesus declared, "I tell you the truth, **no one can see the kingdom of God unless he is born again**" (John 3:3).

*Note: Younger children may memorize the shorter version of this verse in **bold** print.*

Bible Basis:

Luke 22:47—23:49

Bible Truth:

Jesus loves us so much that he died for us.

You Will Need:

- [ ] Game Show Wheel
- [ ] Game Show envelope board
- [ ] 1 poster board
- [ ] butcher paper
- [ ] index cards, markers
- [ ] paper
- [ ] scissors
- [ ] glue sticks
- [ ] large cross drawn on butcher paper
- [ ] half sheets of black construction paper
- [ ] double-stick tape
- [ ] *On the Fast Track! #11* take-home paper
- [ ] *StationMaster Card #11*
- [ ] *(Optional)* treasure box
- [ ] *(Optional)* snack: pretzel sticks, mini-marshmallows
- [ ] *(Optional)* Activity #1: flying disks
- [ ] *(Optional)* Activity #2: self-hardening clay or balsa strips, glue, sharp pointed tool, plastic lanyard or leather strips, scissors, paint and brushes

 GET SET!

(Lesson Preparation)

- ■ Print today's Bible memory verse on a poster board: **Jesus declared, "I tell you the truth, no one can see the kingdom of God unless he is born again" (John 3:3).** Hang the poster board on the wall.
- ■ Create a set of cards that spell out the verse. Write in large letters, one or two words per card, for the Bible Memory Activity.
- ■ Photocopy *On the Fast Track #11* for each child.
- ■ Photocopy *StationMaster Card #11* for each helper.
- ■ Draw and cut out from butcher paper or poster board a large cross shape. Mount on the wall or on an easel for the Welcome Time Activity if using it. (Alternately, draw a large [three feet tall or larger] cross outline on a whiteboard.)
- ■ Make tape lines at either end of the playing area if using Activity #1.
- ■ Set out the Game Show Wheel, Game Show envelope board, and *(optional)* treasure box.
- ■ Set up snack or outside play activities if you include these items in your children's ministry.

 When you see this icon, it means preparation will take more than five minutes.

TICKETS PLEASE!
(Welcome and Bible Connection)

■ *Objective:* To excite children's interest and connect their own life experiences with the Bible Truth, children will create a self-portrait and talk about how Jesus knows and loves us individually.

Welcome Time Activity: Amazing Love

■ *Materials:* *large cross cut out of butcher paper or poster board, markers, paper, scissors, glue sticks*

As children arrive, invite them to draw a self-portrait on paper, making it as detailed as possible. They'll cut it out and glue it on the cross, writing their name near it. As they draw, talk with the children about how personal Jesus is—he knows everything about them and loves them more than a parent or any friend.

Sharing Time and Bible Connection

Introduce today's lesson by discussing these questions with your students. As you talk, give every child the opportunity to say something.

■ **What does it mean to sacrifice something?** (to give it up for the good of someone else)

■ **What are some things you or someone you know has sacrificed?** (giving up free time to help someone, not eating dessert so someone else could have it, letting someone else take your place in line while you go to the back, etc.)

■ **What is the biggest sacrifice you think you could make for someone you love?**

After this sharing time, help your students connect their discussion to the Bible story they are about to hear from Luke 22.

Way before you and I were born, God had a plan for us. He knew we would need forgiveness for all we would do wrong. His plan meant someone had to be the sacrifice for us. Let's find out what God's plan was.

ALL ABOARD FOR BIBLE TRUTH
(Bible Discover and Learn Time)

Luke 22:47–23:49

■ **Objective:** *Children will study Luke 22 and 23 to understand that Jesus suffered and died as their personal sacrifice for sin.*

■ **Materials:** *large cross drawn on butcher paper, half sheets of black construction paper, double-stick tape*

Post the cross at the front of the story area. Hand out a half sheet of black paper to each child.

This black paper will help us see how much Jesus suffered because he loves us. As you hear what bad things happened to Jesus in this story, tear off a piece of paper. You can make a pile in front of you as you listen.

All along we've been finding out who Jesus is and the amazing, exciting things he did while he was living on earth. Think about the people who Jesus made well. Let children remind you who he healed. **And he even brought dead people back to life, like Lazarus. But of all the things Jesus did while he was living on earth, the thing we're going to learn about now was the main reason he came.**

After Jesus ate the Last Supper with his disciples, he was arrested by Jewish leaders. Prompt kids to tear off a piece of black paper. As the story progresses, prompt them as needed. **They wanted to kill Jesus because they were jealous and afraid of him. Everything that was happening was part of God's plan to save you and me from the punishment for our sins.** Ask children for examples of sin.

After Jesus was arrested, he was treated really badly. Soldiers beat him with sticks and whips. They spit on him and called him names and made fun of him. No one stood up for him or said that Jesus didn't deserve any of this wrong treatment. The Jewish leaders wanted to find a person in power who could say that Jesus was a criminal and should be killed. Not one powerful person could find anything at all wrong in what Jesus had done. Do you know why? Allow responses. **Because Jesus had never sinned! He was God so he was without any sin. That's what makes him different from you and me. We've all done things wrong.** Ask children for examples.

Finally, the Jewish leaders got their way. Roman soldiers led Jesus to a hill with two criminals. They made Jesus carry a really heavy wooden cross that was bigger than he was. Someone had to help him because it was so heavy. The soldiers didn't believe Jesus was God's Son. They put nails in his hands and feet to hold him to the cross. It was an awful way to die. Jesus was willing to let this happen because he loves you and me so much. Jesus could have stopped it whenever he wanted to, but he knew this was the way we could be saved from dying for our own wrongs.

After hanging on the cross and being made fun of, Jesus died. When he died, God was so sad, he made the sun stop shining for a while. He caused an earthquake to shake the earth, and he made a huge curtain in the Jewish temple tear in half, right down the middle.

See all those black scraps in front of you? Jesus suffered a lot because you and I have done wrong. We've done lots more wrong than just that many bits of paper. **Let's add those black pieces to the cross.** Direct children to come up in small groups to stick their scraps on the cross. You and helpers should also stick on scraps.

As sad and painful as this day was when Jesus died, something totally huge and wonderful was going to take place next. We'll have to save that part of the story for next week.

As we look at our cross and see all the blackness covering it, we can imagine how much Jesus suffered. <u>We can also see that we have lots of wrongs to be paid for. That's why Jesus died.</u>

Close the story time with prayer, attentive to the Holy Spirit's directing. Pray that those children who haven't decided to ask Jesus to forgive their sins will see how much he loves them and why he died for them.

Use the Clues!
(Bible Review)

Okay, let's see what you remember. Show the Game Show Wheel. **Every week after our story we'll take turns spinning the Game Show Wheel. The color the wheel stops at shows what color question you'll answer. If you spin the "bonus" or "special" sections, you get to do something fun plus answer a question for double points.**

- **Why was Jesus arrested?** (Jewish leaders felt jealous and afraid of him, they wanted to get rid of him)
- **How did Jesus suffer before he died?** (he was beaten, spit on, called names, whipped, made to carry the heavy cross, nailed to the cross)
- **Why did Jesus die?** (to pay for the sins we've done, to give us a chance to spend forever in heaven)
- **How do we decide that we want Jesus' suffering and death to be the payment for our sin?** (we realize we can't fix our sins ourselves, tell Jesus we're sorry for all our wrongs, accept his forgiveness, learn to live life God's way)
- **According to the memory verse, what needs to happen so we can live in heaven forever?** (we need to be born again, be saved, accept Christ, choose to follow Jesus)
- *(Review question)* **What did Jesus leave us as a reminder of his death for us?** (the Last Supper, Communion)

Every bit of punishment and suffering that Jesus felt wasn't what he deserved. You and I deserve the punishment because we have all sinned. Jesus allowed the Jewish leaders and Roman soldiers to hurt him and kill him because he loves you and me so much.

BIBLE MEMORY WAYPOINT
(Scripture Memory)

John 3:3

- ■ **Objective:** *Children will hide God's Word in their hearts for guidance, protection, and encouragement.*
- ■ **Materials:** *verse phrase cards*

Lay out the verse cards on the floor in the shape of a cross. Read the words as you point to them.

Jesus declared, "I tell you the truth, no one can see the kingdom of God unless he is born again" (John 3:3).

Have children take turns reading the words in the cross as you direct by pointing. Remove a card or two and have the group recite the verse. Continue this way, removing (or letting volunteers remove) a card or two. Once the cards are all gone, give children opportunities to put them back in order.

PRAYER STATION

- ■ **Objective:** *Children will explore and practice prayer for themselves in small groups.*
- ■ **Materials:** *Copies of* StationMaster Card #11 *for each adult or teen helper*

Break into small groups of three to five children. Assign a teen or adult helper to each small group and give each helper a copy of *StationMaster Card #11* (see Resources) with ideas for group discussion and prayer.

SNACK STOP: CROSS STICKS (Optional)

If you plan to provide a snack, this is an ideal time to serve it.

- ■ **Materials:** *pretzel sticks, mini-marshmallows*

Provide each child with a small handful of pretzel sticks and several mini-marshmallows. They can use the marshmallows to join pretzel segments together to make symbols (such as crosses and hearts) that go with today's story.

Note: Always be aware of children with food allergies and have another option on hand if necessary

APPLICATION

■ **Objective:** *Children will have opportunities to show how the lesson works in their own lives through activities and take-home papers.*

Some children's ministries may allow children to play outside at this point. If yours does not, choose one of the following activities.

 ## Lifesaver Game

■ **Materials:** *one flying disk per team*
Divide into teams. Each team chooses one player as the "lifesaver." Give each lifesaver a flying disk and send them to the opposite end of the play area. The rest of the teams remain behind the line on their end of the room. **All of your team, except the person with the flying disk, needs to be saved. The only way to be saved is for the person with the life ring (flying disk) to pull you to the other side of the room. You have to hold onto the life ring to get there.** Start the game at your signal; each lifesaver will race to his team and choose a player to take hold of the life ring. Together they'll race back to the other end.
How is this game like what Jesus did for us? (only he can save us)

 ## Cross Necklaces

■ **Materials:** *self-hardening clay or balsa strips, glue, sharp pointed tool, plastic lanyard or leather strips, scissors, paint and brushes*
Guide students in forming a cross from self-hardening clay or two lengths of balsa wood. Painting is an option if there is time. Make a hole near the top of the cross. Fold the lanyard/leather in half; thread the loop through the hole back to front and pull the loose ends through, then tighten. Knot the ends together. Students can wear as a necklace or hang in their rooms as a reminder.

 ## ON THE FAST TRACK! *(Take-Home Papers)*

■ **Materials:** On the Fast Track! #11, *treasure box*

(Optional) Introduce the treasure box by asking: **Who would like to choose a prize from the treasure box?** Anticipate excited responses. Show *On the Fast Track!* take-home papers. **When you take this *On the Fast Track!* paper home each week and do the activities, your parents can sign the ticket that you finished the work. Bring the signed ticket back to choose a prize from the treasure box.** Distribute the take-home papers just before children leave.

LESSON TWELVE: Jesus—Alive Again!

Memory Verse:

If you confess with your mouth, **"Jesus is Lord,"** **and believe in your heart** that God raised him from the dead, **you will be saved (Romans 10:9).**
*Note: Younger children may memorize the shorter version of this verse in **bold** print.*

Bible Basis:

Mark 15:42—16:8; Luke 23:50—24:12

Bible Truth:

Jesus showed us his power when he rose from the dead.

You Will Need:

- [ ] Game Show Wheel
- [ ] Game Show envelope board
- [ ] 1 poster board
- [ ] hand weights
- [ ] foam, golf, tennis, balls and baseballs
- [ ] 7 plastic take-apart eggs
- [ ] Bibles
- [ ] pins or whole cloves
- [ ] toothpicks
- [ ] cinnamon sticks
- [ ] string
- [ ] linen scrap
- [ ] breath mints or mint candy
- [ ] short nails
- [ ] clay or play dough
- [ ] blindfold
- [ ] bowl or basket
- [ ] white piece of cloth

- [ ] gold cording
- [ ] paper towels
- [ ] paper with "RISEN" on it
- [ ] *On the Fast Track! #12* take-home paper
- [ ] *StationMaster Card #12*
- [ ] *(Optional)* treasure box
- [ ] *(Optional)* snack: crispy rice treats in tomb shapes, large marshmallows
- [ ] *(Optional)* Activity #1: a large plastic garbage can with lid per team, bungee cords or duct tape, plastic traffic-type cones or chairs
- [ ] *(Optional)* Activity #2: chairs, sheets, blankets, or tarps

When you see this icon, it means preparation will take more than five minutes.

GET SET!
(Lesson Preparation)

- ■ 🕐 Print today's Bible memory verse on a poster board: **If you confess with your mouth, "Jesus is Lord," and believe in your heart that God raised him from the dead, you will be saved (Romans 10:9).** Hang the poster board on the wall.
- ■ 🕐 Fill the plastic eggs as listed below. Write each egg's number on a piece of tape stuck to the outside.
  - Egg #1: several toothpicks wrapped in linen cloth or paper towel
  - Egg #2: whole spices such as cloves, cinnamon sticks
  - Egg #3: clay or play dough
  - Egg #4: leave empty
  - Egg #5: bright white piece of cloth and piece of gold cording
  - Egg #6: paper with "RISEN" on it
  - Egg #7: folded piece of linen cloth or paper towel

  Place eggs in a bowl or basket when numbered and filled.
- ■ Photocopy *On the Fast Track #12* for each child.
- ■ Photocopy *StationMaster Card #12* for each helper.
- ■ Set out the Game Show Wheel, Game Show envelope board and *(optional)* treasure box.

- Set up snack or outside play activities if you include these items in your children's ministry.
-  Make homemade crispy rice marshmallow treats, shaping the warm confection into a three-sided "tomb" shape that can sit on the table, with an opening about marshmallow size.

TICKETS PLEASE!
(Welcome and Bible Connection)

- **Objective:** *To excite children's interest and connect their own life experiences with the Bible Truth, children will experiment with different equipment and talk about what's powerful.*

Welcome Time Activity: Power Plays

- **Materials:** *hand weights; foam, golf, tennis balls, and baseballs*
  As children arrive, invite them to a table where they can experiment with items that require power. Let them try lifting different hand weights and blowing various balls (foam, golf, tennis, baseball) across the table. Talk about powerful things like volcanoes, superheroes, and huge earth-moving vehicles as you focus on the theme of power.

Sharing Time and Bible Connection

Introduce today's lesson by discussing these questions with the students. As you talk, give every child the opportunity to say something.

- **What is the most powerful thing you've ever seen?**
- **What gives something or someone power?** (muscles, steam, fuel, energy)
- **How powerful do you think God is?**

After this sharing time, help your students connect their discussion to the Bible story they are about to hear from Mark 15—16 and Luke 23—24.

We've all seen cartoons or books where superheroes move huge things and show their strength. But even if these superheroes were real, they wouldn't have as much power as God. Only God could do things like make the earth, cause the sun to move, and bring a dead person back to life. That's why God let Jesus die—because he knew he would bring Jesus back to life. That's how powerful God is. Let's see what happened.

ALL ABOARD FOR BIBLE TRUTH   Mark 15:42–16:8; Luke 23:50–24:12
(Bible Discover and Learn Time)

- **Objective:** *Children will study Mark 15—16 and Luke 23—24 to find out how Jesus came back to life after he was crucified.*
- **Materials:** *7 numbered, filled plastic eggs (see* Get Set!*), Bibles*

Place the bowl of eggs in front of you or, if seated in a circle, in the center.

Ask an older child to pair up with one or more younger children. Form small groups, each with one or more Bibles. Older children can help younger ones find the passages as needed. For each passage, ask a volunteer to read the verse(s), then other children in the group will find and open the corresponding egg. The group with the egg can try to explain how the contents relate to the verse. Discuss the question after each Scripture text.

- *Egg #1: Luke 23:50–53* **What do you think Joseph believed about Jesus?**
- *Egg #2: Luke 23:54–56* **What were these women planning to do with their spices?**
- *Egg #3: Luke 24:1–2* Have child with egg use his or her index finger and thumb to form a "hole" to the burial "tomb." Push the clay "stone" to close the entrance of the "tomb." **Who moved the stone?**
- *Egg #4: Luke 24:3* **Why is this egg empty?**
- *Egg #5: Luke 24:4–5* **Where did these men come from?**
- *Egg #6: Luke 24:6–7* **What had happened by the third day Jesus was in the tomb?**
- *Egg #7: Luke 24:8–12* **What amazed Peter?**

Lots of people were surprised at what happened the third day after Jesus was crucified. Jesus knew he would be alive again after he was killed. But his friends didn't understand how that could happen. That's why they were sad and afraid. They didn't really understand what kind of power Jesus had. <u>But Jesus showed all of us his power by rising from the dead</u>.

Use the Clues!
(Bible Review)

Okay, let's see what you remember. Show the Game Show Wheel. **Every week after our story we'll take turns spinning the Game Show Wheel. The color the wheel stops at shows what color question you'll answer. If you spin the "bonus" or "special" sections, you get to do something fun plus answer a question for double points.**

■ **Where was Jesus buried after he was taken from the cross?** (in a tomb carved out of a cliff or hill)

■ **How do you think Joseph, the women, and Peter felt when they thought Jesus was dead?** (sad, lonely, scared, confused)

■ **How did they feel at the tomb?** (terrified, surprised, excited, happy, amazed)

■ **Who had the power to bring Jesus to life?** (God)

■ **What does the memory verse say we must do to be saved?** (confess with your mouth that Jesus is Lord and believe that God raised him from the dead)

■ *(Review question)* **Why did Jesus allow himself to be crucified?** (to save us, to be the sacrifice for our sin, because he loves us)

BIBLE MEMORY WAYPOINT   Romans 10:9
(Scripture Memory)

■ *Objective: Children will hide God's Word in their hearts for guidance, protection, and encouragement.*

Read this week's memory verse from the poster. Point to each word as you read it:

If you confess with your mouth, "Jesus is Lord," and believe in your heart that God raised him from the dead, you will be saved (Romans 10:9).

Ask the children to help you create gestures and motions to go with the verse. After practicing the motions together as you say the verse, try replacing the words with gestures, such as "mouth," "heart," and "raised." Ask various groups (girls, boys, second-graders, blondes, etc.) to recite the verse with the actions.

PRAYER STATION

- **Objective:** *Children will explore and practice prayer for themselves in small groups.*
- **Materials:** *Copies of* StationMaster Card #12 *for each adult or teen helper*

Break into small groups of three to five children. Assign a teen or adult helper to each small group and give each helper a copy of *StationMaster Card #12* (see Resources) with ideas for group discussion and prayer.

SNACK STOP: EMPTY TOMBS (Optional)

If you plan to provide a snack, this is an ideal time to serve it.

- **Materials:** *crispy rice marshmallow treats in tomb shapes, large marshmallows*

Give each child a "tomb" and marshmallow. Ask them to show you the main facts about the resurrection story, using their snack as props.

Note: Always be aware of children with food allergies and have another option on hand if necessary.

APPLICATION

- **Objective:** *Children will have opportunities to show how the lesson works in their own lives through activities and take-home papers.*

Some children's ministries may allow children to play outside at this point. If yours does not, choose one of the following activities.

Tombstone Roll

- ■ *Materials: one large plastic garbage can with lid per team, bungee cords or duct tape, plastic traffic-type cones or chairs*
  Set up a relay with traffic cones or chairs. Create an oval course (depending on room size). Firmly attach the trash can lid with bungee cords or tape. Depending on size of the trash can, have one child or a pair working together push and roll the can around the traffic cone course and back to the starting point. To make the game more challenging, have the cones/chairs in a spaced-out row, with players maneuvering the can back and forth between the cones to reach the end before rolling it straight back to the starting line.

 Tomb Building

- ■ *Materials: chairs, blankets, sheets or tarps*
  Provide sheets, blankets, or tarps and let the children build a cavelike tomb. Large classes can divide into smaller groups to build separate tombs. Use chairs as the structures on which you drape the sheets. Have children create a way to close their tomb. They can dramatize the Bible story if there is time.

 ON THE FAST TRACK! *(Take-Home Papers)*

- ■ *Materials:* On the Fast Track! #12, *treasure box*

(Optional) Introduce the treasure box by asking: **Who would like to choose a prize from the treasure box?** Anticipate excited responses. Show *On the Fast Track!* take-home papers. **When you take this *On the Fast Track!* paper home each week and do the activities, your parents can sign the ticket that you finished the work. Bring the signed ticket back to choose a prize from the treasure box.** Distribute the take-home papers just before children leave.

LESSON THIRTEEN: Jesus—Coming Again!

Jesus Is Returning!

Memory Verse:

If I go and prepare a place for you, **I will come back and take you to be with me** that you also may be where I am **(John 14:3)**.

*Note: Younger children may memorize the shorter version of this verse in **bold** print.*

Bible Basis:

Acts 1:9–11;
1 Thessalonians
4:15–17; 5:1–2

Bible Truth:

Jesus is coming again!

You Will Need:

- [ ] Game Show Wheel
- [ ] Game Show envelope board
- [ ] 1 poster board
- [ ] CD player
- [ ] music CD
- [ ] sturdy paper plates
- [ ] pizza box (or box of similar size and shape)
- [ ] Bibles
- [ ] Detective Fact Sheets
- [ ] *On the Fast Track!* #13 take-home paper
- [ ] *StationMaster Card* #13
- [ ] (Optional) treasure box
- [ ] (Optional) snack: cotton candy or vanilla pudding, bugle-shaped snacks, paper plates, spoons
- [ ] (Optional) Activity #1: Game Show Wheel (modified), Game Show envelope board, photocopied questions from pages 88–91, baseball diamond
- [ ] (Optional) Activity #2: white cardstock or 4" x 6" unlined index cards, scissors, pencils, markers, string or yarn in 8" lengths, plastic container lids, hole punch, cloud templates

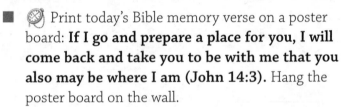

GET SET!
(Lesson Preparation)

- ■ 🕐 Print today's Bible memory verse on a poster board: **If I go and prepare a place for you, I will come back and take you to be with me that you also may be where I am (John 14:3).** Hang the poster board on the wall.
- ■ Photocopy *On the Fast Track #13* for each child.
- ■ Photocopy *StationMaster Card #13* for each helper.
- ■ Photocopy the Detective Fact Sheets, one per every four students, from page 85.
- ■ Set out the Game Show Wheel, Game Show envelope board, and (optional) treasure box.
- ■ Set up snack or outside play activities if you include these items in your children's ministry.
- ■ Photocopy and cut out questions on pages 88–91 if using Activity #1. Place in game envelopes after the Bible Review.
- ■ 🕐 Create a baseball diamond with three bases, home plate, and pitcher's mound, either room-size or tabletop, if using Activity #1.
- ■ 🕐 Cut the centers out of the plastic lids to make hanging rings for the cloud mobiles, if using Activity #2. Cut the string into 8" lengths, five lengths per child. Create a cloud template using the pattern on page 87. If desired, make a sample mobile before class.

When you see this icon, it means preparation will take more than five minutes.

TICKETS PLEASE!
(Welcome and Bible Connection)

■ **Objective:** *To excite children's interest and connect their own life experiences with the Bible Truth, children will experience surprise by playing Freeze Frames to music.*

Welcome Time Activity: Freeze Frames

■ **Materials:** *CD player, music CD*

As children arrive, involve them in a game of Freeze Frames. Play the music CD as children move in random or designated ways (hopping, pretending to swim, swaying, etc.). Explain that when the music suddenly stops, they have to freeze in place. Turn off the music at random times and see who has frozen fastest and in the most unusual positions. Ask children if the stopping of the music surprises them. Chat about other situations when the children have been surprised.

Sharing Time and Bible Connection

Introduce today's lesson by discussing these questions with your students. As you talk, give every child the opportunity to say something.

■ **When you were playing Freeze Frames, were you surprised when the music stopped?**
■ **Do you like surprises, like a surprise visit from someone special?**
■ **What do you think will happen on the day Jesus comes back to earth?**

After this sharing time, help your students connect their discussion to the Bible story they are about to hear from Acts 1 and 1 Thessalonians 4—5.

If you've ever had a really great surprise, then you can start to imagine the excitement and amazement we're going to feel when Jesus comes back here from heaven. He's been planning for that day ever since he went back to heaven. Let's find out what will happen when <u>Jesus comes again</u>.

ALL ABOARD FOR BIBLE TRUTH
(Bible Discover and Learn Time)

Acts 1:9–11;
1 Thessalonians 4:15–17; 5:1–2

- **Objective:** *Children will study Acts 1 and 1 Thessalonians 4—5 to discover that Jesus promised to come again.*
- **Materials:** *Bibles, Detective Fact Sheets from page 85, pencils*

Divide the class into two, four, or six mixed-age groups. Assign each group one of the Bible passages: Acts 1:9–11 or 1 Thessalonians 4:15–17; 5:1–2. **You are going to be detectives, finding out facts about what happened to Jesus after he rose from the dead and what will happen when he comes here again.** Hand out the Detective Fact Sheets, pencils, and Bibles.

Explain that there may be questions that can't be answered by some groups. Have helpers circulate to assist the groups as they read, discuss, and write down what they find.

When groups have finished their detective work, ask them to share their findings. Have all groups covering one passage share their facts, then move on to another passage. When the groups have finished reporting, summarize:

After he came back to life, Jesus spent a little time with his disciples. Then he went back to heaven. He just went straight up into the clouds as the disciples watched. Two angels told the disciples <u>Jesus would come back</u> the same way he left.

Jesus promised he would come back. He said the day would come as a total surprise to everyone. It will be like a thief coming in the middle of the night when no one expects it. There will be a loud voice of an angel and a trumpet sounding. Everyone who has trusted in Jesus as their Savior will go to be with him in heaven.

Even though we can't plan on any certain day or time, we know that <u>Jesus promised to come again</u>, and he will.

Use the Clues!
(Bible Review)

Okay, let's see what you remember. Show the Game Show Wheel. **Every week after our story we'll take turns spinning the Game Show Wheel. The color the wheel stops at shows what color question you'll answer. If you spin the "bonus" or "special" sections, you get to do something fun plus answer a question for double points.**

- **How did Jesus get back to heaven?** (he rose up from the earth and disappeared into the clouds)
- **What will be clues that Jesus has come again?** (a loud command, trumpet sound, we will see him in the clouds)
- **How can we be sure we will see Jesus again?** (he promised to come again, and he keeps all his promises)
- **If the date he's coming back is a surprise, how can we get ready for it?** (expect it to happen at any time, always be following God so we will be ready to go to heaven at that second)

■ **According to the memory verse, what did Jesus promise?** (he would come back and take us to be with him)
■ *(Review question)* **From what we've** learned in the past 12 weeks, tell something Jesus taught us. Accept reasonable answer.

BIBLE MEMORY WAYPOINT
(Scripture Memory)

John 14:3

■ *Objective:* Children will hide God's Word in their hearts for guidance, protection, and encouragement.
■ *Materials:* sturdy paper plates, pizza boxes (or boxes of similar shape and size)

Read this week's memory verse from the poster. Point to each word as you read it:

If I go and prepare a place for you, I will come back and take you to be with me that you also may be where I am (John 14:3).

Recite the verse together several times. Then play a game to further their memorization. Break into small groups for time or class-size needs. For each group, have a helper hold a pizza box 6-10 feet away from the students. One student says the first phrase of the verse. If correct he tosses the paper plate flying disk into the box. If he's wrong, he passes the plate to the next student, who tries. After about five students have recited the first phrase, players must add the next phrase of the verse before earning a chance to toss the plate. Continue adding verse parts until the whole verse is recited. Try to let each child have a chance to recite the entire verse for a chance to fling the plate.

PRAYER STATION

- **Objective:** *Children will explore and practice prayer for themselves in small groups.*
- **Materials:** *Copies of* **StationMaster Card #13** *for each adult or teen helper*

Break into small groups of three to five children. Assign a teen or adult helper to each small group and give each helper a copy of *StationMaster Card #13* (see Resources) with ideas for group discussion and prayer.

SNACK STOP: CLOUDS AND TRUMPETS (Optional)

If you plan to provide a snack, this is an ideal time to serve it.

- **Materials:** *cotton candy or vanilla pudding, bugle-shaped snacks, paper plates, spoons*

Let children create a cloud of cotton candy or pudding (on a plate) and pretend to blow trumpets with the bugle-shaped snacks. Talk about the kinds of things we might be doing when we hear and see Jesus come back.

Note: Always be aware of children with food allergies and have another option on hand if necessary.

APPLICATION

- **Objective:** *Children will have opportunities to show how the lesson works in their own lives through activities and take-home papers.*

Some children's ministries may allow children to play outside at this point. If yours does not, choose one of the following activities.

Jesus Baseball

■ **Materials:** *Game Show Wheel (modified), Game Show envelope board, photocopied questions from pages 88–91, baseball diamond*

Use the Game Show Wheel for a quarter review game. Photocopy and cut out the questions on pages 88–91 and place in the envelope slots in any order. Set up a baseball diamond—either a room-sized one if space allows, or a tabletop one with tokens for players—with bases for first, second, third, and home, plus a pitcher's mound. Modify the Game Show Wheel by writing "1," "2," "3," "out," "foul/spin again," and "free walk" on sticky notes and adhering each to a different color. Children can take turns as pitcher for their team, spinning the wheel. Choose a question based on the color selected. If a team answers a question right, it can move to the appropriate base depending on the message on the color. A wrong answer means the other team gets a turn. Play until the cards are used up or to a certain point number.

Mobile

■ **Materials:** *white cardstock or 4" x 6" unlined index cards, scissors, pencils, markers, string or yarn in 8" lengths, plastic container lids, hole punch, cloud templates on page 87*

Children will create a mobile of clouds as a reminder that Jesus promised to come back to earth, and he could come anytime. Using pre-made templates or by freehand design, children will trace and cut out three or four cloud shapes on cardstock and punch one hole in the top center of each shape. They will write, "Jesus is coming again" on the clouds however they choose. They will tie one end of a length of string or yarn to the plastic circle and put the other through the hole in a cloud. Repeat this step for each cloud, tying each to a string attached to the lid. Make a hanger by tying the end of one additional string to the lid on opposite sides.

ON THE FAST TRACK! *(Take-Home Papers)*

■ **Materials:** On the Fast Track! #13, *treasure box*

(Optional) Introduce the treasure box by asking: **Who would like to choose a prize from the treasure box?** Anticipate excited responses. Show *On the Fast Track!* take-home papers. **When you take this *On the Fast Track!* paper home each week and do the activities, your parents can sign the ticket that you finished the work. Bring the signed ticket back to choose a prize from the treasure box.** Distribute the take-home papers just before children leave.

Kindness Bingo—
For use with lesson 5

Detective Fact Sheet—*For use with lesson 13*

WHO was there?

WHAT happened?

WHERE did it happen?

WHAT was said?

Game Show Wheel and Envelope Board Instructions—*For use with all lessons*

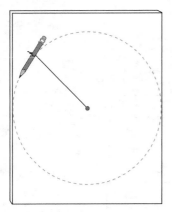

■ *Materials: two or three 12" x 18" white foam-core sheets, string, box cutter, pen or round pencil, 2 rubber bands, large paper clip, markers, yardstick, six 3⅝" x 6½" envelopes, pushpins or stapler*

1. On one foam-core sheet, draw as large a circle as possible. Find the center of the board. Make a single knotted loop at one end of the string and attach to the center with a pushpin. Make a simple compass by extending the string to one long side of the board. Tie a loop and insert the pencil in the loop and tighten, so the pencil will draw a line very close to the edge of the board. Keeping the string taut, draw a circle with the pencil. Remove the pushpin and string. Cut out the circle with the box cutter as carefully as possible. (An uneven circle will not spin well.)

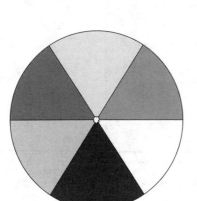

2. Divide the circle into six equal pie-shaped triangles. Color each a different color and use a black marker to draw a border between each color. For best results, place lighter colors between darker ones. Push the pencil or pen through the center of the board and move around to widen the hole slightly.

3. Tightly place a rubber band on the pencil where it emerges from the back of the board, then push the pencil through the center of the second board. The rubber band will hold the two sections slightly apart for better spinning. Place the large paper clip over the pencil in the front of the colored wheel, then tightly place a second rubberband around the pencil in front of the paper clip to hold it in place. The paper clip will be the pointer to indicate the color when the wheel stops spinning. If desired, add two small signs labeled "special" and "bonus" to any two colors on the wheel. When the pointer lands on one of these, the child who spun the wheel will be given an additional "task" to earn extra points.

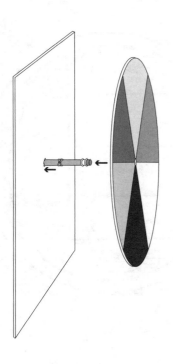

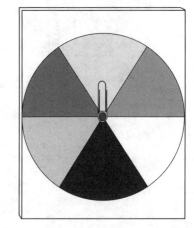

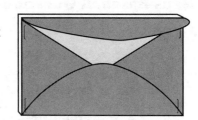

4. To create the Game Show Wheel envelope board, color each of the six envelopes to match the six colors of the wheel. You will have one envelope per color. Staple or tack to a decorated bulletin board or an additional foam-core board, with the open side out. Each week photocopy and cut apart the review questions found in the Use the Clues! section of the lesson. Insert one into each colored envelope.

5. To use the board, have a child spin the wheel. The color the pointer is on when the wheel stops is the color of the envelope from which to take a review question. If there is a "special" or "bonus" sign on that color, the child must also do the task assigned as well as answer the question. Then double points will be awarded. Decide before the quarter begins how many points a correctly answered question will be worth (such as 25 or 100 points).

6. Make an additional set of cards for the "bonus" and "special" tasks. Pull one at random when a "bonus" or "special" sign is indicated. You can use these ideas for tasks or make up your own:
   —shake the hands of all the teammates
   —rub your tummy while patting your head
   —turn around three times and shout, "hallelujah"
   —do five jumping jacks
   —run in place for 30 seconds
   —sing "Happy Birthday" to the child next to you
   —flap your arms like a chicken and crow like a rooster

- -

Cloud Templates—*For use with lesson 13*

Jesus Baseball Questions—*For use with lesson 13*

Q. What did Jesus show us about pleasing God and our parents?

A. To listen, obey, and respect our parents, to grow in our spirits and learn about God, to live his way.

Q. Why did Jesus stay behind in Jerusalem when he was 12, when his parents couldn't find him on their trip back home?

A. He wanted to please God, his heavenly Father, by learning more from the Jewish teachers in the temple.

Q. A mother of two grown sons asked Jesus to give her sons the places of honor in heaven. How did Jesus answer her?

A. Her sons were going to suffer like he would, but only God could give out places of honor. The first will be last, and the one who serves is the greatest of all.

Q. How did Jesus show us how to serve?

A. He healed people, he gave his life for us, he served those around him, he spent time with sinners.

Q. When Jesus healed 10 lepers, who thanked him?

A. Just one man who was healed.

Q. After hearing about the leper who said thank you, how should we act because God has done great things for us?

A. Praise and thank God for all he does.

Q. What did Jesus teach us by caring for two blind men and giving them ability to see again?

A. To show kindness to others.

Q. What did the blind men do after Jesus cured their blindness?

A. They followed Jesus.

Q. Why was the rich man who built bigger barns for his crops called foolish?

A. Because he hoarded and held onto his stuff instead of using it as God would want; he was selfish, he loved his stuff more than God.

Q. How do we store up treasure in heaven?

A. By using our stuff to honor God, sharing it with those in need, giving instead of keeping things to ourselves, serving God.

Q. Why did Jesus show mercy to the lame man near the pool?

A. Because he cared about him. He knew God loved the man, he saw something he could do for a needy person and did it.

Q. Since we can't heal people, how can we show mercy?

A. Spend time with people in need, do what we can for them, share what we have with them, don't ignore or mistreat those who are sick or disabled.

Jesus Baseball Questions—*For use with lesson 13*

Q. What two commandments did Jesus say we should live by?

A. Love God with all your heart, soul, mind, and strength, and love your neighbor as yourself.

Q. How do we show God we love him?

A. Talk to him often, obey him, read his Word, do the things that please him.

Q. Why did Mary pour her expensive perfume on Jesus' feet?

A. To show him honor, to demonstrate her love and respect for him.

Q. How can we honor Jesus today?

A. Praising him, thanking him for all he does for us and gives us, giving tithes and offerings cheerfully, working at whatever we do with our best effort. Love him before anyone or anything else.

Q. How do we remember what Jesus did when he died for us?

A. By celebrating the Last Supper/Communion.

Q. What do the bread and wine/juice stand for in the Last Supper/Communion?

A. The bread stands for Jesus' body broken for us, and the wine/juice for his blood that paid for our sin.

Q. Why was Jesus crucified if he had never done anything wrong and was guilty of no crime?

A. Because his death was a sacrifice to pay for our sins. It was part of God's plan to make us free of sin and able to one day live with him in heaven.

Q. How can we have our sins forgiven?

A. By asking Jesus to forgive our sins and believing that he is God's Son, and that he died in our place; trusting that his death paid for the wrongs we've done.

Q. How did Jesus show his immeasurable power?

A. He rose from the dead.

Q. On the third day after Jesus died, what did the women who were coming with spices to Jesus' tomb find?

A. The stone that closed the tomb was rolled back, the cloth that was wrapped around Jesus' body was empty, and an angel who told them that he was alive again.

Q. What important promise did Jesus make before he went back to heaven?

A. He would come again.

Q. How will Jesus come again?

A. In the clouds, suddenly, with a trumpet blast and loud voice.

Dear Parents,

During the next thirteen weeks in children's ministry, your child will learn about the life of Jesus. Our *Lead the Way, Jesus* curriculum examines the life of Jesus in an exciting and interactive way while also giving children an opportunity to build lifetime habits of prayer. Your child will explore why and how people pray and will learn to pray in small groups.

Lead the Way, Jesus uses the **imPACT** model of prayer to help children understand the four important activities of prayer—praise, ask, confess, and give thanks. Here are some discussion questions you may use at home to reinforce your child's growing desire to talk with God:

- *Praise.* Ask your child: **What do you really like about God?** Listen to the responses. Then say: **Let's tell God we like these things about him.** Encourage your child to tell God directly what he or she likes about him.

- *Ask.* It is important for children to know that God cares about their needs. We can ask God to help us, our families, and our friends with any problems. He wants everyone to ask him for what they need. Ask: **What would you like to ask God?** Let your child name some prayer requests. Then say: **Let's tell God about these needs.** Take turns praying for these needs.

- *Confess.* Tell your child that we all do things we wish we didn't do. Sometimes our actions or words hurt someone and then we are sorry. Ask: **What's one thing that you wish you didn't do this last week?** Listen to the response. Then say: **Let's confess our sin to God and tell him we're sorry.** Together, bow heads and confess this sin before God.

- *Give thanks.* Ask: **What are some things that you're thankful that God has done for you or has given to you?** Listen to the responses. Then say: **Let's tell God thank you for these things.** Take turns thanking God.

Since prayer is such an important concept, your child will receive a take-home paper for each lesson, designed to support the Bible Truth for that day. These take-home papers will include fun activities, a Bible memory verse, and a prayer challenge. Some of the activities invite the involvement of the whole family. Encourage your child to complete these activities and bring the signed *On the Fast Track!* ticket the following Sunday.

If you have any questions about this study, please feel free to discuss them with the children's ministry leaders. We are excited about what God is going to do in the lives of our children. We would appreciate your prayers for the teachers and children.

In His Name,

Children's Ministry Coordinator

Dear Children's Ministry Helper,

Welcome to *Discipleship Junction!* During the next 13 weeks, you will play a major role in the lives of children as you teach them about the life of Jesus and pray with them in small groups. The *Lead the Way, Jesus* curriculum will help you build habits of prayer into their lives that will last a lifetime as they learn to follow Jesus. The **imPACT** model of prayer will remind children about the four important activities of prayer: praise, ask, confess, and give thanks.

■ *Praise.* Ask: **What do you really like about God?** Let volunteers briefly respond, then say: **Let's tell God we like these things about him.** Help children talk to God directly.

■ *Ask.* Ask children: **What would you like to ask God?** Allow children to give prayer requests, then say: **Let's tell God about these needs.** It is important for children to know that God cares about everyone's needs. Have them take turns praying for the needs in their lives.

■ *Confess.* We all do things we wish we didn't do. Sometimes our actions or words hurt someone and then we are sorry. Ask them: **What's one thing that you wish you didn't do this last week?** Give children time to answer, then say: **Let's confess our sins to God and tell him we're sorry.**

■ *Give thanks.* When giving thanks, ask your group: **Tell one thing that you're thankful that God has done for you.** Let children share, then say: **Let's tell God thank you for these things.**

The children's ministry appreciates the important role that you have volunteered to fill. We are confident that God is going to do amazing things in the lives of our children.

Sincerely,

Children's Ministry Coordinator

StationMaster Card #1

This week your group learned from Luke 2:41–52 that *like Jesus, we can grow up pleasing God and our parents.* Lead your group in prayer in the following way:

■ *Praise.* **Jesus lived on earth so he could be an example for us.** Have students praise Jesus for living just like us so we could have his example to follow.

■ *Ask.* **Jesus chose to always obey Mary and Joseph. As you ask God's help in obeying your parents, tell him one area you want to learn to better obey in.**

■ *Confess.* **Jesus did what his parents asked. Is there an area in which you did not obey your parents this week?** Lead students in asking God's forgiveness for a specific wrongdoing.

■ *Thank.* **Jesus loves you so much that he was willing to become a child too.** Model thanking Jesus for showing us how to grow up to please God and our moms and dads.

Remember that no child should be forced to pray, but do encourage and invite each one to participate. When you've finished praying, you can quietly talk to the children in your group until the next activity.

StationMaster Card #2

This week your group learned from Matthew 20:20–28 that *like Jesus, we can serve others with caring hearts.* Lead your group in prayer in the following way:

■ *Praise.* **Jesus is worth praising because he shows us how to serve the way he did.** Let students praise God with phrases or sentences as they choose.

■ *Ask.* **To be great in God's kingdom, you must be the least. We can do that only with God showing us how.** Lead students to ask God for wisdom on how they can put others first.

■ *Confess.* **Like James and John, we sometimes** want the best for ourselves, but that's not Jesus' way. Let's spend a minute telling God about the times we have recently thought only of ourselves, and ask his forgiveness. Lead students in asking for forgiveness.

■ *Thank.* **Because Jesus came to serve instead of be served, he died in our place. Let's thank him for that sacrifice.** Allow time for children to thank God, either aloud or silently.

Remember that no child should be forced to pray, but do encourage and invite each one to participate. When you've finished praying, you can quietly talk to the children in your group until the next activity.

StationMaster Card #3

This week children learned from Luke 6:43–45 that *Jesus wants us to know and live the truth.* Lead your group in prayer in the following way:

■ *Praise.* **Jesus is called the Way, the Truth, and the Life.** Have students praise Jesus using these and similar titles.

■ *Ask.* **To learn to live truthfully we need God's help.** Have students ask God to help them grow truthful inside and out.

■ *Confess.* **It's so easy to say less than the truth, or act in a way that isn't honest. We all are** tempted to do that. Give students time to confess dishonest words and deeds.

■ *Thank.* **God is so patient with us as we work on being truthful inside and out. We shouldn't forget to thank him for his Spirit living in us to teach us to live his way.** Allow students to thank God as they choose.

Remember that no child should be forced to pray, but do encourage and invite each one to participate. When you've finished praying, you can quietly talk to the children in your group until the next activity.

StationMaster Card #4

This week children learned from Luke 17:11–19 that *we owe Jesus gratefulness and praise*. Lead your group in prayer in the following way:

- *Praise.* **Jesus has done many miracles and answered many prayers. What has he done for you?** Have students praise God for a personal answered prayer or help in time of need.
- *Ask.* **The 10 men with leprosy asked Jesus for help. Nothing is too hard for God to do.** Give students time to present their concerns and needs to the Father.

- *Confess.* **Remember how only one healed man thanked Jesus? We don't thank him often enough for his help, care, and protection.** Model for children how to tell God they're sorry for times they've forgotten to be thankful to him.
- *Thank.* **Right now you can tell God thank you for anything you want.** Allow students to thank God however they choose.

Remember that no child should be forced to pray, but do encourage and invite each one to participate. When you've finished praying, you can quietly talk to the children in your group until the next activity.

StationMaster Card #5

This week we learned from Matthew 20:29–34 that *like Jesus, we can show kindness*. Lead your group in prayer in the following way:

- *Praise.* **You and I have been shown kindness by Jesus too. Let's praise him for how he is so loving and caring toward us.** Lead students in sentence praises.
- *Ask.* **When we're not sure how to show kindness, we can be sure God will give us ideas.** Have children ask God to give them practical ideas on showing kindness this week.
- *Confess.* **Many people are unkind to or just ignore people who are different than**

themselves. That saddens God. Lead children in confessing times they remember having not been kind to people, especially those with disabilities or differences.
- *Thank.* **Let's tell God thank you for loving us even with our differences and weaknesses.** Give children an opportunity to thank God as they are led by the Spirit.

Remember that no child should be forced to pray, but do encourage and invite each one to participate. When you've finished praying, you can quietly talk to the children in your group until the next activity.

StationMaster Card #6

This week your group learned from Luke 12:15–21 that we need to *love God more than our stuff*. Lead your group in prayer in the following way:

- *Praise.* **Instead of wanting more stuff, let's practice praising God for all we have.** Lead children in praising God for their homes, possessions, family, friends, etc.
- *Ask.* **The rich man in the story never asked God how to use his stuff wisely. We can do that so we're not foolish like he was.** Help children talk to God about using what they have for the benefit of others.
- *Confess.* **We can get greedy for more and jealous of the things others have.** Give children an opportunity to ask forgiveness for wrong attitudes and actions regarding their possessions.
- *Thank.* **God loves to hear us thank him for blessing us.** Model for children a prayer of thanks for blessing them with good things.

Remember that no child should be forced to pray, but do encourage and invite each one to participate. When you've finished praying, you can quietly talk to the children in your group until the next activity.

StationMaster Card #7

This week your group learned from John 5:2–9 that *like Jesus, we can show mercy*. Lead your group in prayer in the following way:

- *Praise.* **When Jesus was on earth, he healed people's bodies. He also showed them compassion and encouraged them to have faith in God.** Have students praise God for being able to heal our bodies and also to save us.
- *Ask.* **One way you can show mercy to a sick person is to ask God to heal or help him or her.** Let students pray for people they know who are sick or disabled. Pray for their salvation if they don't know Jesus.
- *Confess.* **Sometimes it is hard to trust God when we, or people we love, are sick for a long time.** Allow time for students to confess silently or aloud a lack of belief, or any other wrong they're aware of.
- *Thank.* **God made our bodies with wonderful care. We've all been sick sometime and have gotten better.** Lead students in sentence prayers of thanksgiving for health, the fun they can enjoy with their bodies, and healing they or someone else has experienced recently from illness or injury.

Remember that no child should be forced to pray, but do encourage and invite each one to participate. When you've finished praying, you can quietly talk to the children in your group until the next activity.

StationMaster Card #8

This week your group learned from Matthew 22:35–40 that we should *love Jesus first, and others next*. Lead your group in prayer in the following way:

- *Praise*. **Jesus deserves our love because he first loved us.** Have children praise Jesus as their Savior and friend.
- *Ask*. **When we don't know how to show love to God or to someone else, God knows what we can do. You can ask him right now for his ideas on how to follow Jesus' two commandments**.
- *Confess*. **Can you think of a time you thought of yourself first and didn't even remember to show love to God or to someone else? We're all guilty of that sometimes.** Model a prayer of confession for children that they can repeat or use as a start of their own confession.
- *Thank*. **God shows us love every day. Other people do too.** Ask children to think about who has shown love to them, and thank God for the person.

Remember that no child should be forced to pray, but do encourage and invite each one to participate. When you've finished praying, you can quietly talk to the children in your group until the next activity.

StationMaster Card #9

This week your group learned from John 12:1–8 that *we honor Jesus with our best*. Lead your group in prayer in the following way:

- *Praise*. **Jesus is worthy of our honor and praise. Mary honored him with perfume. We honor him with our words of praise and worship.** Model a sentence prayer for the children to encourage them to praise the Lord and worship him with their words.
- *Ask*. **Sometimes doing our best to obey is what honors Jesus.** Have children ask God to help them obey in specific situations they find hard or frustrating.
- *Confess*. **We don't always give our best, and that dishonors the Lord.** Lead children in asking forgiveness for instances of choosing to give less than their best.
- *Thank*. **What can you thank God for today? Think of the ways he has blessed or helped you.** Allow children to offer thanks to God as they choose.

Remember that no child should be forced to pray, but do encourage and invite each one to participate. When you've finished praying, you can quietly talk to the children in your group until the next activity.

StationMaster Card #10

This week your group learned from Luke 22:7–20 that by celebrating the Last Supper *we remember what Jesus did for us.* Lead your group in prayer in the following way:

- *Praise.* **God knew when he created the whole earth that one day his Son, Jesus, would come here to die for us.** Have children praise God for his plan to send Jesus.
- *Ask.* **Jesus wanted his disciples and us to know about the forgiveness of sins. Maybe you're thinking of a friend or family member who hasn't decided to follow Jesus. You can ask Jesus to make himself known to that person.** Lead children in praying for unsaved friends and family.

- *Confess.* **Jesus told his disciples that the best leader serves others. He wanted them to be willing to be a servant. Serving can be hard or even lonely.** Have students ask God to forgive them for any times they haven't served like they should.
- *Thank.* **Even when he was soon going to be hurt and killed, Jesus was thinking of us.** Lead students in prayers of thanksgiving for giving us a way to remember what he did for us.

Remember that no child should be forced to pray, but do encourage and invite each one to participate. When you've finished praying, you can quietly talk to the children in your group until the next activity.

StationMaster Card #11

This week your group learned from Luke 22:47—23:49 that *Jesus loves us so much that he died for us.* Lead your group in prayer in the following way:

Note: Be sensitive to the possibility that one or more children may be ready to pray to accept Christ.

- *Praise.* **Jesus suffered and died for our sins.** Have children praise Jesus for his sinless life and example to us.
- *Ask.* **Jesus sacrificed his life for us. If you want to ask Jesus to forgive your sins and become your Savior and friend, you can do that right now.** Pray a simple prayer of salvation that children can pray aloud or silently.
- *Confess.* **Even after we've trusted Jesus to be our Savior, we do wrong and need his forgiveness. We can tell him about what we've done wrong this week and ask him to clean away those wrongs and give us a new start.** Lead children in a prayer of confession.
- *Thank.* **Jesus suffered and died so every person could be with God for eternity.** Allow children to thank God for preparing a place for them.

Remember that no child should be forced to pray, but do encourage and invite each one to participate. When you've finished praying, you can quietly talk to the children in your group until the next activity.

This week your group learned from Mark 15:42—16:8 and Luke 23:50—24:12 that *Jesus showed us his power when he rose from the dead.* Lead your group in prayer in the following way:

- *Praise.* **God planned from the beginning of the world to make a way for us to live forever. Let's praise him for thinking of us before we were born.** Lead the children as they praise God however they desire.
- *Ask.* **Jesus' power is something we can see at work in our own lives. If you know of a need for God to use his power, you can ask him now.** Give children opportunity to talk to God about a need.
- *Confess.* **Any wrongs we've done this week will keep us from having a close friendship with God. He wants to forgive your sins, if you'll tell him about them.** Allow children to confess their wrongs silently or aloud.
- *Thank.* **Heaven will be our home one day because Jesus was willing to die for us. Let's thank him.** Lead children in expressing thanks.

Remember that no child should be forced to pray, but do encourage and invite each one to participate. When you've finished praying, you can quietly talk to the children in your group until the next activity.

StationMaster Card #13

This week your group learned from Acts 1:9–11; 1 Thessalonians 4:15–17; and 5:1–2 that *Jesus is coming again!* Lead your group in prayer in the following way:

- *Praise.* **Jesus is looking forward to us being with him in the place he's prepared for us. Let's praise him as our King and Lord who's going to share heaven with us.** Lead children in praise to God.
- *Ask.* **Sometimes waiting for Jesus to come back is difficult, or the idea of leaving our lives here can be scary.** Have children ask God to help them be cheerful and do whatever he asks of them while they wait for his return.
- *Confess.* **Do you forget that God has left us here for a while to live for him until Jesus comes again?** Give children time to confess anything they need to.
- *Thank.* **Jesus promised to come again, because he wants us to join him in heaven.** Thank Jesus that we can count on him keeping every promise he makes.

Remember that no child should be forced to pray, but do encourage and invite each one to participate. When you've finished praying, you can quietly talk to the children in your group until the next activity.

On the Fast Track!

 ## Prayer Challenge

Have you ever been lost? How did you feel? This week, pray for someone you know who is lost because he or she doesn't know God, our heavenly Father. Pray for this person by name every day or night this week with your family. Ask God to help this person come to Jesus as his or her Savior.

Think and Do

Twelve pennies are hidden in this haystack. Search for them like Mary and Joseph searched for Jesus. Circle or color them.

Your Turn

Be a good example like Jesus! Write or draw a picture of three ways you can be a good example to those around you. Then do each one this week.

By using your words:

By using your actions:

 ## Memory Verse

Teach me your way, O LORD, and I will walk in your truth (Psalm 86:11).

In your thoughts:

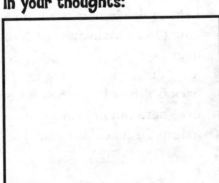

Dear Parents and Guardians,

Please check off the items your child completed this week:

❏ Prayer Challenge
❏ Memory Verse
❏ Your Turn
❏ Think and Do

Adult Signature:
_____

FAST TRACK! TICKET

On the Fast Track!

Prayer Challenge

If you made a servant headband in class, let it remind you to pray that God will bless whomever you serve this week. Tell your parent who you prayed for and served.

Memory Verse

Serve wholeheartedly, as if you were serving the Lord, not men (Ephesians 6:7).

Your Turn

Try being a secret servant. Find at least one way to serve someone when that person can't see you. You might pick up litter around a neighbor's house or sneak into a brother's or sister's room to clean up. Or take out the trash when your mom or dad is out of the room.

Attitude Matters

How does God desire us to serve him and others? Search for the following words hidden in the puzzle.
CARE, KIND, HELP, LOVE, SERVE, BLESS, AID, SUPPORT

S	U	P	P	O	R	T
E	L	K	R	P	N	C
R	O	A	I	D	S	A
V	V	Q	B	N	T	R
E	E	N	Z	X	D	E
H	E	L	P	I	P	R
T	V	B	L	E	S	S

Dear Parents and Guardians,

Please check off the items your child completed this week:

☐ Prayer Challenge
☐ Memory Verse
☐ Your Turn
☐ Attitude Matters

Adult Signature:

_____

FAST TRACK! TICKET

On the Fast Track!

Prayer Challenge

God values clean hearts. Confessing our wrongs to him is a good habit to learn. Each day this week, before you ask God for anything, ask him to help you remember untruthful words or actions you've done. When his Spirit helps you remember them, tell God you're sorry and ask his forgiveness.

Memory Verse

Your word is truth (John 17:17).

Your Turn

Practice spotting truth and untruthfulness. When you watch television or a movie, or read a story, look for the people who show they are living the truth (good fruit) by the way they talk and act. Also look for those who are not living the truth (bad fruit) by their words and actions. Tell your parents what you observed.

Truth Crossword

Find where these words for good fruit fit into the crossword puzzle:

truth
sincere
honest
fair

honorable
trustworthy
integrity

Dear Parents and Guardians,

Please check off the items your child completed this week:

❏ Prayer Challenge
❏ Memory Verse
❏ Your Turn
❏ Truth Crossword

Adult Signature:

_____

FAST TRACK! TICKET

On the Fast Track!

Prayer Challenge

Talk with your family about someone in your home or elsewhere who's experienced a miracle from God. Ask him or her to tell you what happened. As a family, have a time of prayer when you thank God and praise him for doing this miracle.

Memory Verse

Give thanks to the LORD, for he is good. His love endures forever (Psalm 136:1).

Mystery Picture

This mystery picture shows one way to praise God for his miracle-working power. Color in the parts with two dots to reveal the picture.

Your Turn

Put a jar or cup in a central place at home, with a bunch of pennies or pebbles next to it. As you learn to be thankful to God every day, drop a penny or pebble into the jar each time you thank him. Be thankful for big things and small things (like finding a lost item or playing with a friend). See how full the jar is by the end of the week.

Dear Parents and Guardians,

Please check off the items your child completed this week:

- ☐ Prayer Challenge
- ☐ Memory Verse
- ☐ Your Turn
- ☐ Mystery Picture

Adult Signature:

_____

FAST TRACK! TICKET

On the Fast Track!

Prayer Challenge

Sometimes our friends are mean or unkind. Sometimes a complete stranger is unkind to us. Our job as followers of Jesus is to be kind regardless. It is harder to be kind to someone who is mean than to someone who is kind. This week you can pray for one person who has been unkind to you or others.

Memory Verse

Make sure that nobody pays back wrong for wrong, but **always try to be kind to each other and to everyone else** (1 Thessalonians 5:15).
*Note: Younger children may memorize the shorter version of this verse in **bold** print.*

Follow Jesus Maze

Follow Jesus through the maze to reach the blind men.

Your Turn

Did you make a Kindness Bingo card in class? If so, use it this week. If you didn't make one, choose someone in your neighborhood or school who is not kind to you. Ask your parents to help you make cookies, paint a picture, or invite that child to play at your house. Do this act of kindness because Jesus is always kind to you.

Dear Parents and Guardians,

Please check off the items your child completed this week:

- ☐ Prayer Challenge
- ☐ Memory Verse
- ☐ Your Turn
- ☐ Follow Jesus Maze

Adult Signature:

FAST TRACK! TICKET

On the Fast Track!

Prayer Challenge

Do you make "wish lists" for gifts you would like for Christmas or your birthday? This week, start a "wish list" of treasures in heaven you want to build. Ask God each day to show you how to build a treasure in heaven. Watch for how God answers your prayer. Share what you're learning with your family.

Memory Verse

Store up for yourselves treasures in heaven...for **where your treasure is, there your heart will be also (Matthew 6:20-21).**

*Note: Younger children may memorize the shorter version of this verse in **bold** print.*

Your Turn

The next time you have a chance to buy something you want, or a grown-up is willing to buy it for you (clothes, toys, treats), choose something that is less expensive or pass up the item altogether. Use the savings to offer to God for what pleases him (a special offering at church, school supplies for needy kids, homeless shelter food). Maybe your example will cause others to choose to love God more than their stuff.

Acrostic Poem

Make an acrostic poem. Write a word or phrase about storing up your treasures where they count most. Use what you learned in class and in your memory verse. The first two have been done for you.

T hings aren't the most important
R iches are in heaven
E
A
S
U
R
E

Dear Parents and Guardians,

Please check off the items your child completed this week:

❏ Prayer Challenge
❏ Memory Verse
❏ Your Turn
❏ Acrostic Poem

Adult Signature:

FAST TRACK! TICKET

On the Fast Track!

Prayer Challenge

Pray for someone who has a long-term illness or disability, such as a person who is blind, deaf, or paralyzed. If that person doesn't know Jesus, pray he or she will receive the gift of Jesus' love and forgiveness for his or her sins. Pray God would show his compassion to this person in a way he or she can understand and that he or she will have joy and not be discouraged.

Memory Verse

"The King will reply, 'I tell you the truth, **whatever you did for one of the least of these brothers of mine, you did for me'** " (Matthew 25:40).

Note: Younger children may memorize the shorter version of this verse in **bold** *print.*

Healing Words

Find where these words from today's lesson fit into the puzzle:

compassion, care, pray, save, encourage, love, faith, heal

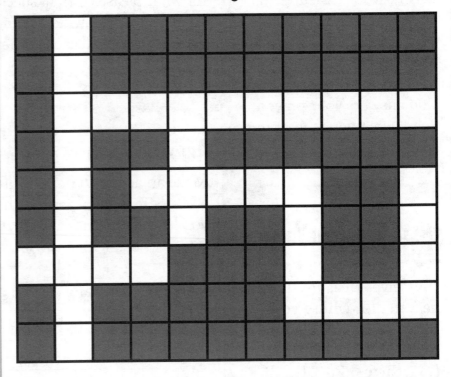

Your Turn

Try to find out what it's like to need mercy. With your parent's help, choose an experiment below or make up your own.

- Eat only rice and water for a day to see what it's like to go hungry.
- Keep one arm inside your shirt all day on Saturday to see what it's like to be disabled.
- Sleep on the hard floor with just a blanket (no pillow) to see what it's like to be homeless.

Dear Parents and Guardians,

Please check off the items your child completed this week:

- ☐ Prayer Challenge
- ☐ Memory Verse
- ☐ Your Turn
- ☐ Healing Words

Adult Signature:

_____

FAST TRACK! TICKET

Prayer Challenge

Each day as you pray this week, tell God a new reason you love him. With a parent, pray for a chance to show love to someone new each day this week.

Memory Verse

He answered: "'**Love the Lord your God with all your heart and** with all your **soul and** with all your **strength and** with all your **mind**'; and '**Love your neighbor as yourself**'" (Luke 10:27).

Note: Younger children may memorize the shorter version of this verse in **bold** *print.*

Snail Crawl

Start at the first letter in the snail shape. Move slowly like a snail, blacking out every b, g, and m. When you reach the center, go back to the start and write the letters to see what the message says.

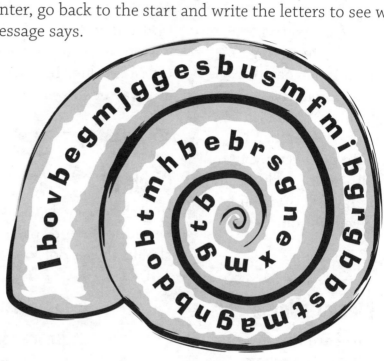

__ ___ _____ ____ ___ ____

____ _____ _____ _____.

Your Turn

If you made a Love Bag in class, ask your parent for help in filling it and seeking out someone to give it to. If you've been praying for a way to show love to someone each day, God will make it clear who you can give your Love Bag to. If you didn't make a bag in class, decorate a paper lunch sack and fill it with things that would be helpful to someone: a street person, lonely senior citizen in a nursing home, child in a hospital, etc.

Dear Parents and Guardians,

Please check off the items your child completed this week:

- ❑ Prayer Challenge
- ❑ Memory Verse
- ❑ Your Turn
- ❑ Snail Crawl

Adult Signature:

_____

FAST TRACK! TICKET

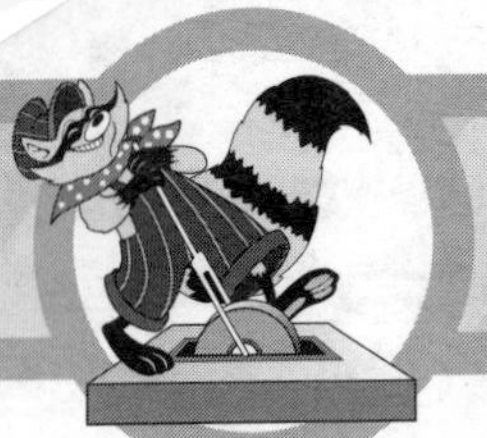

On the Fast Track!

Prayer Challenge

Choosing to spend some of your time talking to God is one way to show honor to him. Decide on a time you will spend one minute talking to God (praying) each day this week: first thing in the morning, before breakfast, at lunch, before dinner, before bed. You can do this on your own or with your family. Each time you pray, tell God you want to give him your best.

Memory Verse

"You are worthy, our Lord and God, to receive glory and honor and power, for you created all things, and by your will they were created and have their being" (Revelation 4:11).

Note: Younger children may memorize the shorter version of this verse in **bold** *print.*

Your Turn

Think of something you do well, such as draw or play an instrument or play a sport. Use that ability in some way that honors God this week. Draw a picture on a card and write an encouraging note to a teacher or pastor. Learn a new song to share at church or a Christian club. Teach a younger child a sport or activity as a way of showing care.

Circle It

In each row, circle the word that does not rhyme. Then write those words on the lines below to learn what we should always do!

greater, later, Creator, honor

poor, sore, Jesus, more

with, true, glue, flew

dot, your, caught, blot

grow, snow, best, blow

_____ _____ _____

_____ _____ .

Dear Parents and Guardians,

Please check off the items your child completed this week:

❏ Prayer Challenge
❏ Memory Verse
❏ Your Turn
❏ Circle It

Adult Signature:

_____

FAST TRACK! TICKET

Prayer Challenge

We often forget to thank Jesus. Each day, whenever you eat a meal this week, thank him for something besides the food. Thank him for your family, eternal life, your friends, being safe, good health, and other things you think of.

Memory Verse

The Word became flesh and made his dwelling among us. We have seen his glory, the glory of the One and Only, who came from the Father, full of grace and truth **(John 1:14).**

*Note: Younger children may memorize the shorter version of this verse in **bold** print.*

Your Turn

This week recreate the Last Supper with your family. It can be before a meal or after dinner. Use simple crackers if you don't have matzo or pita bread, and grape juice for the wine. Tell what Jesus did and what the bread and wine stand for. End by thanking Jesus for leaving us such a great reminder of his sacrifice.

Word Scramble

Think of the Last Supper. Remember who and what was there. Unscramble the words that tell about that night.

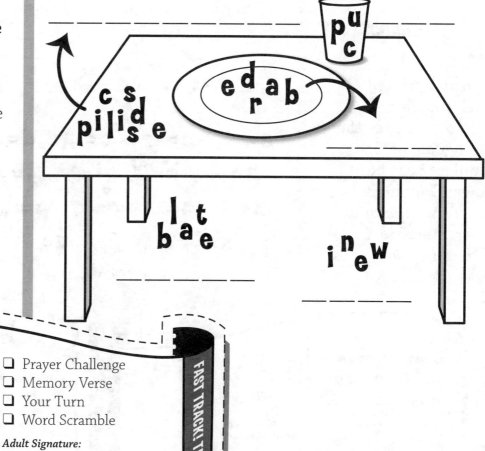

Dear Parents and Guardians,

Please check off the items your child completed this week:

- ☐ Prayer Challenge
- ☐ Memory Verse
- ☐ Your Turn
- ☐ Word Scramble

Adult Signature:

FAST TRACK! TICKET

On the Fast Track!

Prayer Challenge

Jesus gave up his life to pay for our sins. This week, ask God each day to show you any sins you've done. Once you remember them, ask Jesus to forgive you for each one. This practice of confession is part of living life Jesus' way.

Memory Verse

Jesus declared: "I tell you the truth, **no one can see the kingdom of God unless he is born again**" (John 3:3).

*Note: Younger children may memorize the shorter version of this verse in **bold** print.*

Your Turn

The only way to have your life cleaned up from sin is to ask Jesus for forgiveness. He can forgive you because he suffered and died for you. This week, ask your mom or dad for three ways you can help clean up at home: wash dishes, give your pet a bath, vacuum, help with laundry, sweep, or some other job. Cleaning can remind you of how Jesus cleans our hearts from sin because he died for us.

Decode the Message

What's another way to say you have trusted in Jesus as your Savior? Decode the words by finding what letter each symbol stands for. Write the letter on the line above the symbol. Then talk to your mom or dad about what the words mean.

Dear Parents and Guardians,

Please check off the items your child completed this week:

❏ Prayer Challenge
❏ Memory Verse
❏ Your Turn
❏ Decode the Message

Adult Signature:

FAST TRACK! TICKET

On the Fast Track!

Prayer Challenge

As you pray this week, praise Jesus for his awesome power. Tell him ways his power makes a difference to you. Pray with a parent if you need help thinking of ways to praise Jesus for his mighty power.

Memory Verse

If you confess with your mouth, **"Jesus is Lord,"** and believe in **your heart** that God raised him from the dead, **you will be saved** (Romans 10:9).
*Note: Younger children may memorize the shorter version of this verse in **bold** print.*

Resurrection Search

There are seven words about Jesus coming back to life hidden in the picture. Find and circle the words.

Your Turn

On a sheet of paper, write *Praise* at the top. During the week, try to find as many things as you can that bring praise to God. Draw a picture or write each thing on your sheet. You might praise God for seeing the first butterfly this season or for hamburgers, a favorite tree, or your brother. Try to make your Praise paper as attractive as possible. You can hang it in your room as a reminder that God is good.

Dear Parents and Guardians,
Please check off the items your child completed this week:

- ❑ Prayer Challenge
- ❑ Memory Verse
- ❑ Your Turn
- ❑ Resurrection Search

Adult Signature:

_____

FAST TRACK! TICKET

On the Fast Track!

Prayer Challenge

Thank God for preparing a place for you in heaven. Write down names of friends and family who don't know Jesus. Pray by name for them to choose to follow Jesus as their Savior before he comes again.

Memory Verse

If I go and prepare a place for you, **I will come back and take you to be with me** that you also may be where I am **(John 14:3).**

*Note: Younger children may memorize the shorter version of this verse in **bold** print.*

Color-by-number Picture

Color the picture below using the following colors: 1=yellow, 2=blue, 3=red.

Dear Parents and Guardians,

Please check off the items your child completed this week:

- ❏ Prayer Challenge
- ❏ Memory Verse
- ❏ Your Turn
- ❏ Color-by-number Picture

Adult Signature:

_____

FAST TRACK! TICKET

Your Turn

With a parent or other grown-up, make a poster about heaven. Read Revelation 21 together and draw what heaven will be like. On the poster write, "Jesus is coming again!"